THE ULTIMATE
SAN FRANCISCO GIANTS
TRIVIA BOOK

A Collection of Amazing Trivia Quizzes
and Fun Facts for Die-Hard Giants Fans!

Ray Walker

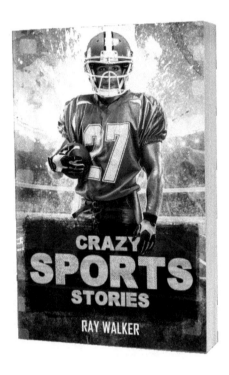

CONTENTS

INTRODUCTION

The San Francisco Giants debuted in 1883 as the New York Gothams. Three years later, they were renamed the New York Giants. They moved out West to San Francisco in the late 1950s. Being one of the most established teams in baseball means they have a storied past with players, teams, and championships aplenty.

The Giants franchise has won eight World Series titles. Their first in San Francisco was in 2010. They then won the World Series every other year through 2014. They were one of the most dominant teams of the 2010s and had personalities who will be remembered by baseball fans for years to come.

The Giants play at Oracle, one of the most beautiful and unique ballparks in the United States. Who wouldn't want to gaze at the gorgeous San Francisco Bay as they eat garlic fries and watch the greatest sport in the world? The Giants have Hall-of-Famers like Willie Mays, Willie McCovey, and Juan Marichal highlighting their captivating past.

The thing about baseball is that it is a lot like life. There are good times and bad times, good days and bad days, but you have to do your absolute best to never give up. The San

Francisco Giants never give up...you can't win three World Series in a decade if you give up.

When the Giants won the 2010, 2012, and 2014 World Series, they accomplished something that not many teams will ever accomplish again. They won 30% of the championships in the decade, even though they were only one of 30 teams. That's not an easy thing to do.

The Giants are one of five teams in California and one of two in the Bay Area. Their nearby rivals, the Los Angeles Dodgers and Oakland A's, are a big part of their history, as well. From the 1989 Bay Bridge World Series to the many instances of drama with the Dodgers, you are sure to be entertained if you are a Giants fan.

So, let's see if you truly bleed orange and black......

CHAPTER 1:

ORIGINS & HISTORY

QUIZ TIME!

1. Which name has the Giants franchise NOT gone by in its history?

    a. New York Gothams

    b. San Francisco Giants

    c. New York Giants

    d. San Francisco Gothams

2. In what year was the Giants franchise established?

    a. 1880

    b. 1883

    c. 1885

    d. 1900

3. Oracle Park (the Giants' current ballpark) was the first privately funded ballpark since Dodger Stadium opened in 1962.

    a. True

    b. False

4. In which division do the Giants currently play?

   a. American League West
   b. American League Central
   c. National League West
   d. National League Central

5. When did construction on Oracle Park begin?

   a. 1997
   b. 1995
   c. 1920
   d. 1877

6. Which ballpark did the Giants NEVER play in?

   a. Candlestick Park
   b. Hilltop Park
   c. Seals Stadium
   d. Levi's Stadium

7. Where did the "Giants" name first originate?

   a. A newspaper nicknamed them the Giants because of their high number of tall players.
   b. Grover Cleveland called them the Giants as a nickname.
   c. Owner John Day wanted to change the team's name.
   d. Manager Jim Mutrie was so overcome after a win that he blurted out that his players were giants.

8. What was Oracle Park originally named?

   a. Oracle Park
   b. Pacific Bell Park

c. SBC Park

d. AT&T Park

9. What is the name of the Giants' Triple-A team, and where are they located?

a. El Paso Chihuahuas

b. Reno Aces

c. Las Vegas Aviators

d. Sacramento River Cats

10. What year did the Giants move from New York to San Francisco?

a. 1958

b. 1957

c. 1941

d. 1945

11. The NFL's San Francisco 49ers also played at Candlestick Park for almost 30 years.

a. True

b. False

12. Which song is played over the loudspeakers after a Giants' win at home?

a. "San Francisco" by Niall Horan

b. "Everywhere You Look" by Jesse Frederick (*Full House* theme song)

c. "I Left My Heart in San Francisco" by Tony Bennett

d. "San Francisco (You've Got Me)" by the Village People

13. Who threw the San Francisco Giants' first no-hitter in 1963?

    a. Juan Marichal
    b. Don Larsen
    c. Gaylord Perry
    d. Frank Linzy

14. Who threw the first perfect game in Giants franchise history in 2012?

    a. Madison Bumgarner
    b. Matt Cain
    c. Tim Lincecum
    d. Barry Zito

15. The NFL's New York Giants were named after the San Francisco Giants franchise, which had once been known by the same name.

    a. True
    b. False

16. What is the name of the Giants' mascot?

    a. Giants Giraffe
    b. Lou Seal
    c. Giants Gorilla
    d. Dolph Dolphin

17. In the fan parking lot at Oracle Park, there are two huge sculptures on display. One is of a baseball glove, and the other is of _____.

a. A batting helmet

b. A Cracker Jack box

c. A Coca-Cola bottle

d. A baseball bat

18. What year did the Giants win their first World Series after moving to San Francisco?

a. 2012

b. 2010

c. 2014

d. 1989

19. Who was the very first manager of the Giants franchise?

a. Bruce Bochy

b. Rogers Hornsby

c. Jim Price

d. John Clapp

20. The Giants franchise has won the most games of any team in the history of American baseball.

a. True

b. False

QUIZ ANSWERS

1. D – San Francisco Gothams

2. B – 1883

3. A – True

4. C – National League West

5. A – 1997

6. D – Levi's Stadium

7. D – Manager Jim Mutrie was so overcome after a win that he blurted out that his players were giants.

8. B – Pacific Bell Park

9. D – Sacramento River Cats

10. A – 1958

11. A – True

12. C – "I Left My Heart in San Francisco" by Tony Bennett

13. A – Juan Marichal

14. B – Matt Cain

15. A – True

16. B – Lou Seal

17. C – A Coca-Cola bottle

18. B – 2010

19. D – John Clapp

20. A – True

DID YOU KNOW?

1. In 2013, the Giants finished in last place, becoming the first team since the 1998 Miami Marlins to finish in last place the year after winning a World Series.

2. After managing the Giants for 13 seasons, Bruce Bochy stepped down as manager in 2019. They won three championships during his tenure.

3. If the ball lands in the bay, it is not just a home run; it is also known as a "Splash Hit."

4. When the Giants arrived in San Francisco, the city threw a parade before the opener at Seals Stadium, former home of the San Francisco Seals. The Giants played at Seals Stadium for two seasons until Candlestick Park opened.

5. Only one MLB All-Star Game has been hosted at Oracle Park so far. The game took place in 2007 and the American League won. The Giants did host two MLB All-Star Games at Candlestick Park, in 1961 and 1984, as well.

6. Players inducted into the National Baseball Hall of Fame as San Francisco Giants include Orlando Cepeda, Juan Marichal, Willie McCovey, and Gaylord Perry.

7. The Giants have had 10 team captains in franchise history, but none since 1984. Those captains were Jack Doyle, Dan McGann, Larry Doyle, Gus Mancuso, Mel Ott, Alvin Dark, Willie Mays, Willie McCovey, Darrell Evans, and Jack Clark.

8. The Giants' home PA announcer is Renel Brooks-Moon. She is the only female PA announcer in all of Major League Baseball.

9. If the Giants are leading after the 8th inning, Journey's "When the Lights Go Down in the City" is played. If the Giants are trailing after the 8th inning, Journey's "Don't Stop Believin'" is played.

10. Duane Kuiper is the Giants' TV announcer. His brother Glen is the TV announcer for the Oakland A's, just across the bay. The Kuiper Brothers are from Wisconsin.

CHAPTER 2:

JERSEYS & NUMBERS

QUIZ TIME!

1. In 2000, the Giants' home jerseys no longer had names on the back and the jersey color changed from white to cream, a color they had used in the past.

   a. True
   b. False

2. Which number is not retired by the Giants (as of the 2019 season)?

   a. 24
   b. 25
   c. 26
   d. 27

3. The New York Giants' colors were brown and blue.

   a. True
   b. False

4. What uniform number does catcher Buster Posey wear?

a. 26

b. 28

c. 34

d. 37

5. What uniform number did Willie Mays wear with the Giants?

a. 22

b. 24

c. 25

d. 29

6. Who is the player whose number was most recently retired by the Giants?

a. Gaylord Perry

b. Monte Irvin

c. Juan Marichal

d. Barry Bonds

7. No Giants player has ever worn the uniform number 0.

a. True

b. False

8. Barry Zito wore number 75 for the Giants. Who is the only other Giant ever to wear number 75?

a. Enderson Franco

b. Jean Machi

c. Dan Otero

d. Joe Nathan

9. Which former Giants legend has his number 44 retired by the team?

    a. Orlando Cepeda
    b. Willie Mays
    c. Willie McCovey
    d. Juan Marichal

10. The Giants are the only MLB team whose colors include both orange AND black.

    a. True
    b. False

11. What are the Giants' official team colors?

    a. Black, orange, metallic gold, white
    b. Black, orange, cream
    c. Black, orange, metallic gold, cream
    d. Black, orange, gray, white

12. Bill Terry spent his entire 14-season playing career with the Giants. He then managed them from 1932-1941. His number ____ was retired by the team in 1983.

    a. 2
    b. 3
    c. 4
    d. 5

13. The Giants wore patches on their jerseys throughout the 2019 season to honor the late Willie McCovey and the late Peter McGowan.

a. True

b. False

14. What number did Carl Hubbell wear as a Giant?

    a. 11

    b. 3

    c. 10

    d. 21

15. Giants catcher _____ was the first catcher to openly wear protective leg gear.

    a. Fred Tenney

    b. Tom Needham

    c. Frank Bowerman

    d. Roger Bresnahan

16. Pitcher Christy Mathewson is retired by the Giants but does not have a number retired because he played for the Giants before they began using numbers on their jerseys.

    a. True

    b. False

17. Shortstop Brandon Crawford currently wears number ____ for the Giants.

    a. 33

    b. 35

    c. 37

    d. 39

18. Pitcher Madison Bumgarner currently wears number ____ for the Giants.

a. 38

b. 40

c. 44

d. 48

19. First baseman Brandon Belt currently wears number _____ for the Giants.

    a. 5

    b. 7

    c. 9

    d. 11

20. What number did pitcher Tim Lincecum wear during his tenure with the Giants?

    a. 50

    b. 53

    c. 55

    d. 58

QUIZ ANSWERS

1. A – True
2. C – 26
3. B – False
4. B – 28
5. B – 24
6. D – Barry Bonds
7. B – False, The number was worn by Al Oliver and Jeffery Leonard.
8. A – Enderson Franco
9. C – Willie McCovey
10. B – False, Baltimore Orioles
11. C – Black, orange, metallic gold, cream
12. B – 3
13. A – True
14. A – 11
15. D – Roger Bresnahan
16. A – True
17. B – 35
18. B – 40
19. C – 9
20. C – 55

DID YOU KNOW?

1. Giants catcher Roger Bresnahan invented the batting helmet. His invention became mandatory for all batters to wear, starting in 1970. He decided to invent the batting helmet because he had been knocked out by a pitch from Reds pitcher Andy Coakley. So, while he recovered, he invented what we all know of today as a batting helmet.

2. The Giants have retired Bill Terry's number 3, Mel Ott's number 4, Carl Hubbell's number 11, Monte Irvin's number 20, Willie Mays's number 24, Juan Marichal's number 27, Orlando Cepeda's number 30, Gaylord Perry's number 36, and Willie McCovey's number 44. Barry Bonds's number 25 is retired by the Giants unofficially because he has not been named to the National Baseball Hall of Fame. Christy Mathewson and John McGraw are also honored but do not have a number retired.

3. In 1916, the New York Giants had four different uniforms. Three out of the four were plaid. The wide plaid look lasted for only one season, then the Giants moved on from it...thankfully. Around this time, teams tended to redesign their uniforms on a seasonal basis.

4. In 1917, the words "New York" across the Giants' road jerseys were in purple. The jersey itself was a cross-hatching design that, once again, lasted for only one season.

5. In 1922, the New York Giants actually wore white and blue pinstripes very much like their foes, the New York Yankees. The year before this was the first all-New York World Series that the Giants won.

6. The Giants debuted the colors we know them for today in 1933—orange and black. Yet these colors only lasted for three seasons until they went back to blue.

7. In 1942, the Giants debuted uniforms with zippers. Many baseball teams were fascinated by the invention and incorporated them into their jerseys. That year, their home uniforms were red, white, and blue because of World War II.

8. In 1978, the Giants wore an alternate pullover jersey that was popular with teams in the '70s and early '80s. This year was also the second year that uniform numbers appeared on the front of the jerseys.

9. In 1904, the Giants wore jerseys that were pullover but had four buttons down the front. The collar was full, which fit in with the uniform style of that time.

10. In 1999, the Giants wore a patch on their sleeves that read "Tell it Goodbye." It was their farewell to Candlestick Park.

CHAPTER 3:

FAMOUS QUOTES

QUIZ TIME!

1. Which beloved Giant once said: "Baseball is a game, yes. It is also a business. But what it most truly is, is disguised combat. For all its gentility, its almost leisurely pace, baseball is violence under wraps."?

   a. Willie McCovey
   b. Willie Mays
   c. Juan Marichal
   d. Bobby Bonds

2. Which former Giants player said: "There are three things in my life which I really love: God, my family, and baseball. The only problem—once baseball season starts, I change the order around a bit."?

   a. Tito Fuentes
   b. Barry Bonds
   c. Willie Mays
   d. Al Gallagher

3. Which former Giants manager is quoted as saying, "If you're not prepared, it's not pressure you feel, it's fear."?

    a. Dusty Baker
    b. Felipe Alou
    c. Bruce Bochy
    d. Alvin Dark

4. After almost being hit by a pitch, which former Giant once said: "They shouldn't throw at me. I have five or six kids."?

    a. Juan Marichal
    b. Tito Fuentes
    c. Barry Bonds
    d. Angel Pagan

5. Which famous actor is quoted as saying: "I've been a Giants fan since I was a kid. Growing up in Sacramento, we didn't have a baseball team of our own, so it was always A's or Giants. And due to my dislike of the designated hitter—and the fact that all my friends were Giants fans—I started young."? (His famous actor dad is an A's fan.)

    a. Patrick Schwarzenegger
    b. Scott Eastwood
    c. Colin Hanks
    d. John Owen Lowe

6. Which Giants announcer is quoted as saying: "The Giants have won. They have won the World Series for the third

time in five years. Madison Bumgarner has firmly etched his name on the all-time World Series record books as one of the best greatest World Series pitchers the game has ever seen."?

a. Jon Miller
b. Duane Kuiper
c. Mike Krukow
d. Lon Simmons

7. Brian Wilson is one of the funniest baseball players of the past decade. Which of the following hilarious quotes did he NOT say?

a. "It smells like eggs in here. Did you fart? Did I fart?"
b. "I'm a certified ninja. It happened in a dream. Normally it takes a lifetime, but I did it in 12 minutes."
c. "That's a clown question, bro."
d. "Chuck Norris has been known to throw a baseball 100 mph. I've been known to throw Chuck Norris 100 mph."

8. Pitcher Gaylord Perry once said, "They'll put a man on the moon before I hit a home run." On July 20, 1969, a couple of hours after Neil Armstrong landed on the moon, Perry hit his first and only home run.

a. True
b. False

9. Which former Giant is quoted as saying: "Winning is the only thing that makes me happy. Ask my wife. I don't get

happy about anniversaries or birthdays. I don't care about that. Just winning."?

a. Barry Bonds
b. Jeff Kent
c. Sergio Romo
d. Matt Williams

10. After the 1989 World Series, which former Giant is quoted as saying: "Hypothetically, if there was no earthquake, I was liking our chances."?

a. Kevin Mitchell
b. Matt Williams
c. Rick Reuschel
d. Will Clark

11. Which former Giant once said: "When people are wrong, you've got to let them know it."?

a. Jeff Kent
b. Will Clark
c. Barry Bonds
d. Orlando Cepeda

12. Which former Giant is quoted as saying: "I was born to hit a baseball. I can hit a baseball."?

a. Barry Bonds
b. Willie Mays
c. Willie McCovey
d. Bobby Bonds

13. Which former Giant once joked: "I could run like a gazelle, couldn't I?"

a. Willie Mays

b. Willie McCovey

c. Orlando Cepeda

d. Mel Ott

14. Which former Giant is quoted as saying: "Every time I sign a ball, and there must have been thousands, I thank my luck that I wasn't born Coveleski or Wambsganss or Peckinpaugh."?

a. Bill Terry

b. George Davis

c. Willie Mays

d. Mel Ott

15. Which former Giants manager is quoted as saying: "Everyone knows something, and nobody knows everything."?

a. Dusty Baker

b. Bruce Bochy

c. Joe Altobelli

d. Cap Anson

16. Giants legend Willie Mays once said, "Never allow the fear of striking out keep you from playing the game."

a. True

b. False

17. Pablo Sandoval is quoted as saying, "It's not about _____. It's about how you treat the player."

a. Money

b. Winning

c. The game

d. The stats

18. Which former Giants pitcher once said: "I refuse to be molded into some stereotypical ballplayer that has no interests, no life, no depth, no intelligence."?

a. Tim Lincecum

b. Juan Marichal

c. Barry Zito

d. Tim Hudson

19. Which former Giants manager said: "Be anything you want to be, but don't be dull."?

a. Jim Davenport

b. Alvin Dark

c. John McGraw

d. Frank Robinson

20. Gaylord Perry once said: "The trouble with baseball is that it is not played the year-round."

a. True

b. False

QUIZ ANSWERS

1. B – Willie Mays

2. D – Al Gallagher

3. C – Bruce Bochy

4. B – Tito Fuentes

5. C – Colin Hanks

6. A – Jon Miller

7. C – "That's a clown question, bro." (Bryce Harper said it.)

8. A – True

9. B – Jeff Kent

10. D – Will Clark

11. D – Orlando Cepeda

12. A – Barry Bonds

13. B – Willie McCovey

14. D – Mel Ott

15. A – Dusty Baker

16. B – False, Babe Ruth said it.

17. A – Money

18. C – Barry Zito

19. D – Frank Robinson

20. A – True

DID YOU KNOW?

1. "This is one you'll want to wear. I wear it all the time. I don't wear jewelry so to speak, but I'll wear this with a lot of pride." – Bruce Bochy, when given his 2010 World Series ring.

2. "They throw the ball, I hit it. They hit the ball, I catch it." – Willie Mays

3. "I think I was the best baseball player I ever saw." – Willie Mays

4. "Ballplayers, like everyone else, like to get told they did something right." – Willie McCovey

5. "Even during my career, when I read all those great things about me, it's almost like I was reading about someone else. It's almost like there was another person." – Willie McCovey

6. "It's called talent. I just have it. I can't explain it. You either have it or you don't." – Barry Bonds

7. "Every pitcher can beat you, it doesn't matter how good you are." – Barry Bonds

8. "People out there said I was too small. It's those kinds of moments that pushed me to be where I'm at right now." – Tim Lincecum

9. "It's a game of inches." – Tim Hudson

10. "Hunter Pence eats pizza with a fork." – Barack Obama

CHAPTER 4:

CATCHY NICKNAMES

QUIZ TIME!

1. Pablo Sandoval's nickname is also an animal. Which animal's name does he go by?

   a. Koala

   b. Fox

   c. Panda

   d. Wolf

2. Willie Mays credits sportswriter Jimmy Cannon with creating his nickname, the "Say Hey Kid."

   a. True

   b. False

3. "Buster" is the nickname of Giants catcher Posey. What is his real first name?

   a. Michael

   b. Brad

   c. Keith

   d. Gerald

4. What is pitcher Madison Bumgarner's nickname?

   a. Bummy
   b. Mad Bum
   c. Maddie Bum
   d. Mr. Bum

5. Which is NOT a nickname commonly applied to the Giants as a team?

   a. The G-Men
   b. Los Gigantes
   c. The Giant Sluggers
   d. The Orange and Black

6. Brandon Belt also has an animal nickname. What is it?

   a. The Baby Giraffe
   b. The Baby Tiger
   c. The Baby Lion
   d. The Baby Goat

7. A baby giraffe at Six Flags Discovery Kingdom was named "Brandon" in honor of Brandon Belt.

   a. True
   b. False

8. Which nickname did Juan Marichal NOT go by?

   a. Manito
   b. J. Mar
   c. Dominican Dandy
   d. Mar

9. During 2017's MLB Player Weekend, what nickname did Giants manager Bruce Bochy have displayed on the back of his jersey?

   a. Manager
   b. BB
   c. Bruce
   d. Boch

10. Pitching legend Randy Johnson played for the Giants for one season in 2009. What is his famous nickname?

   a. The Tall Unit
   b. The Big Unit
   c. The Threatening Unit
   d. The Intimidating Unit

11. "Goose" is a nickname. What is the real name of former Giants pitcher Goose Gossage?

   a. Maxwell William Gossage
   b. Richard Michael Gossage
   c. Kevin Arthur Gossage
   d. Bartholomew Robert Gossage

12. Orlando Cepeda's nickname was "The Babe Cobb of the Dominican."

   a. True
   b. False

13. "Dusty" is a nickname. What is the real first name of former Giants manager Dusty Baker?

a. James

b. Johnnie

c. David

d. Daniel

14. What is former Giants pitcher Derek Holland's nickname?

a. Holly

b. Dutch Oven

c. Dutch Derek

d. Daunting Derek

15. Which former Giants player went by the nickname "Will the Thrill"?

a. Willie Mays

b. Willie McCovey

c. Will Clark

d. Matt Williams

16. What is J.T. Snow's full name?

a. James Thomas Snow Jr.

b. Jonathan Thomas Snow Jr.

c. Jacob Thomas Snow Jr.

d. Jack Thomas Snow Jr.

17. Former Giants pitcher Matt Cain went by the nickname "Cain and Able."

a. True

b. False

18. Former Giants manager Frank Robinson was nicknamed after which office supply?

a. Sharpener

b. Notebook

c. Pencils

d. File folder

19. During 2019's MLB Player Weekend, what nickname did Giants shortstop Brandon Crawford have on the back of his jersey?

a. DJ BC RAW

b. B CRAW

c. CRAWDAD

d. C-FORD

20. What is former Giant Chili Davis's real name?

a. Clarence Theodore Davis

b. Cameron Theodore Davis

c. Charles Theodore Davis

d. Christopher Theodore Davis

QUIZ ANSWERS

1. C – Panda

2. A – True

3. D – Gerald

4. B – Mad Bum

5. C – The Giant Sluggers

6. A – The Baby Giraffe

7. A – True

8. B – J. Mar

9. D – Boch

10. B – The Big Unit

11. B – Richard Michael Gossage

12. B – False, It's "The Babe Cobb of Puerto Rico."

13. B – Johnnie

14. B – Dutch Oven

15. C – Will Clark

16. D – Jack Thomas Snow Jr.

17. B – False

18. C – Pencils (due to his thin stature)

19. A – DJ BC RAW (He is known as the clubhouse DJ and postgame playlist curator.)

20. C – Charles Theodore Davis

DID YOU KNOW?

1. Tito Fuentes's real name is Rigoberto Fuentes Peat. In addition to "Tito," another common nickname of his was "Parakeet" because he was known as one of the most talkative players of his era. He was known for being a chatterbox when he was on base.

2. The Giants' TV broadcasters, Mike Krukow and Duane Kuiper, go by the tandem nickname of "Kruk and Kuip."

3. Former Giants pitcher Ryan Vogelsong went by the simple nickname "Vogey."

4. Barry Bonds was given some brutal nicknames following the accusations that he used performance-enhancing drugs. Among them were "The Hormone King," "The Asterisk," and "The Sultan of Shot."

5. Giants pitcher Jeff Samardzija goes by the nickname "Shark." He got the nickname in college because his teammates thought that he looked like Bruce the Shark from *Finding Nemo*.

6. Outfielder Angel Pagan went by the appropriate, obvious, and punny nickname, "Angel in the Outfield."

7. Willie McCovey often went by the nickname "Stretch" due to his ability to catch high and wide throws at first base.

8. Tim Lincecum went by the nickname "The Freak" because of his crazy athletic abilities.

9. Candlestick Park, former home of the Giants and San Francisco 49ers, was often referred to as "The Stick" by fans and Bay Area residents.

10. "Triples Alley" is the nickname for the large gap in right-centerfield at Oracle Park. When the ball is hit to this area, it almost always leads to a triple for the batter.

CHAPTER 5:

THE SAY HEY KID

QUIZ TIME!

1. What is Willie Mays's middle name?

   a. Edward

   b. James

   c. Howard

   d. John

2. Willie Mays played for only two MLB teams in his career. The New York/San Francisco Giants and the New York Mets.

   a. True

   b. False

3. Where was Willie Mays born?

   a. Albuquerque, New Mexico

   b. Westfield, Alabama

   c. Frisco, Texas

   d. New Orleans, Louisiana

4. When was Willie Mays born?

    a. June 15, 1929

    b. June 6, 1931

    c. May 15, 1929

    d. May 6, 1931

5. Willie Mays never appeared in an MLB All-Star Game.

    a. True

    b. False

6. How many Gold Glove Awards did Willie Mays win?

    a. 12

    b. 29

    c. 10

    d. 8

7. Where did Willie Mays go to high school?

    a. James Clemens High School

    b. Booker T. Washington High School

    c. Westfield High School

    d. Fairfield Industrial High School

8. Before the 1963 season, Willie Mays got a raise in salary that made him the highest played player in baseball.

    a. True

    b. False

9. What year did Willie Mays make his Major League Baseball debut?

a. 1949

b. 1951

c. 1955

d. 1960

10. At 16 years old, Willie Mays joined a team in the Negro American League. Which team did he play for before his contract was purchased by the New York Giants?

a. Philadelphia Stars

b. Indianapolis ABC's

c. Newark Eagles

d. Birmingham Black Barons

11. Willie Mays created a charity to fulfill his dream of giving every child a chance by offering underprivileged youth positive opportunities and safer communities. What is the name of his charity?

a. The Willie Mays Family Foundation

b. The Willie Mays Children Foundation

c. The Say Hey Foundation

d. The Say Hey Kids Foundation

12. Willie Mays was drafted by and served in the army during the Korean War and missed over 200 MLB games. He played baseball for the army, where he learned the basket catch.

a. True

b. False

13. What year was Willie Mays inducted into the National Baseball Hall of Fame?

   a. 1982
   b. 1979
   c. 1990
   d. 1975

14. In 2015, Willie Mays was awarded the Presidential Medal of Freedom by President Barack Obama.

   a. True
   b. False

15. Willie Mays was once banned from the MLB by Commissioner Bowie Kuhn for _____.

   a. Betting on game outcomes
   b. Drinking on the job
   c. Working at a casino
   d. Knowing about other players using steroids

16. What is the title of Willie Mays's memoir that he co-wrote with John Shea?

   a. Forever Giant: 24 Lessons from Willie Mays
   b. 24: Life Stories and Lessons from the Say Hey Kid
   c. Willie Mays: Life Stories and Lessons from the Say Hey Kid
   d. The Say Hey Kid: Life Lessons and Stories from Giants Legend Willie Mays

17. There is a Willie Mays statue in front of Oracle Park at 24 Willie Mays Plaza.

a. True

b. False

18. Willie Mays completed one of the best defensive plays in MLB history. In Game 1 of the 1954 World Series, he made an over-the-shoulder catch while running and threw the ball back to the infield so no runners could advance. What is this specific play by Mays often referred to as?

a. The Play

b. The Throw

c. The Catch

d. The Flip

19. What game show did Willie Mays make an appearance on in 2004 when the show came to San Francisco?

a. Jeopardy

b. Family Feud

c. The Price Is Right

d. Wheel of Fortune

20. Willie Mays is the godfather of former Giants star Barry Bonds.

a. True

b. False

QUIZ ANSWERS

1. C – Howard

2. A – True

3. B – Westfield, Alabama

4. D – May 6, 1931

5. B – False, He played in 24 All-Star Games.

6. A – 12 (And he won them all consecutively.)

7. D – Fairfield Industrial High School

8. A – True

9. B – 1951

10. D – Birmingham Black Barons

11. C – The Say Hey Foundation

12. A – True

13. B – 1979

14. A – True

15. C – Working at a casino

16. B – *24: Life Stories and Lessons from the Say Hey Kid*

17. A – True

18. C – The Catch

19. D – *Wheel of Fortune*

20. A – True

DID YOU KNOW?

1. In September of 2017, MLB renamed the World Series MVP Award the "Willie Mays World Series Most Valuable Player Award." The first such award was won by George Springer of the Houston Astros.

2. Mays loves to travel by air. He is one of only 66 people to hold an American Airlines Lifetime Pass.

3. Mays shares the record for most All-Star Games played at 24 with Hank Aaron and Stan Musial.

4. During his playing days, Willie Mays charged $100 for an interview, then split that money four ways and gave it to the four lowest-paid players on the Giants' roster.

5. Willie Mays was inducted into the California Sports Hall of Fame in 2007 by Governor Arnold Schwarzenegger and First Lady Maria Shriver.

6. May 6th, Willie Mays's birthday, is Willie Mays Day in the state of California.

7. Willie Mays is referred to in John Fogerty's popular song, "Centerfield," and The Treniers recorded a song called "Say Hey (The Willie Mays Song)" in 1955.

8. Willie Mays was referred to multiple times in the comic strip, "Peanuts," by Charles M. Schulz.

9. Willie Mays was a hitting instructor for the New York Mets from 1973-1979.

10. In 1964, Willie Mays became the first African-American team captain for a Major League team.

CHAPTER 6:

STATISTICALLY SPEAKING

QUIZ TIME!

1. Willie Mays holds the Giants franchise record for the most home runs. How many did he hit as a Giant?

   a. 646

   b. 623

   c. 555

   d. 605

2. Pitcher Juan Marichal has the most wins in San Francisco Giants franchise history, with 372.

   a. True

   b. False

3. How many times have the Giants made the playoffs since moving to San Francisco?

   a. 10 times

   b. 18 times

   c. 12 times

   d. 7 times

4. Which former Giant holds the single-season record for doubles, with 49 in 2001?

   a. J.T. Snow
   b. Barry Bonds
   c. Ramon Martinez
   d. Jeff Kent

5. Which pitcher has the most strikeouts in Giants franchise history, with 2,504?

   a. Juan Marichal
   b. Christy Mathewson
   c. Madison Bumgarner
   d. Gaylord Perry

6. Which player has the most RBI in Giants franchise history, with 1,860?

   a. Orlando Cepeda
   b. Barry Bonds
   c. Willie McCovey
   d. Mel Ott

7. Dusty Baker is the Giants' all-time winningest manager.

   a. True
   b. False

8. Which Giant holds the record for the most saves in franchise history, with 206?

   a. Robb Nen
   b. Sergio Romo

   c. Brian Wilson

   d. Santiago Casilla

9. Who holds the Giants franchise record for stolen bases, with 428?

   a. Willie Mays

   b. Mike Tiernan

   c. George Van Haltren

   d. Art Devlin

10. Who holds the single-season Giants record for hits, with 254?

   a. Don Mueller

   b. Freddie Lindstrom

   c. Mike Donlin

   d. Bill Terry

11. Who holds the Giants' record for home runs in a season, with 73?

   a. Barry Bonds

   b. Willie Mays

   c. Kevin Mitchell

   d. Orlando Cepeda

12. Will Clark hit the most sacrifice flies in Giants franchise history.

   a. True

   b. False

13. Who threw the most wild pitches in Giants franchise history, with 222?

a. Tim Lincecum

b. Tim Keefe

c. Red Ames

d. Mickey Welch

14. Who holds the Giants' record for triples in a season, with 27?

    a. Larry Doyle

    b. Buck Ewing

    c. George Davis

    d. Red Murray

15. Who holds the Giants franchise record for being intentionally walked, with 575 (340 more than the player in 2nd place)?

    a. Barry Bonds

    b. Willie Mays

    c. Willie McCovey

    d. Chili Davis

16. Which Giants hitter holds the single-season record for strikeouts, with 189?

    a. Brandon Belt

    b. Matt Williams

    c. Bobby Bonds

    d. Dave Kingman

17. Christy Mathewson has both the most wins and the most losses in Giants franchise history.

    a. True

    b. False

18. Which player has the most plate appearances in Giants franchise history, with a whopping 12,016?

    a. Willie McCovey
    b. Mel Ott
    c. Barry Bonds
    d. Willie Mays

19. Which two former Giants pitchers are tied for most saves in a single season, with 48?

    a. Robb Nen and Brian Wilson
    b. Rod Beck and Brian Wilson
    c. Rod Beck and Robb Nen
    d. Brian Wilson and Sergio Romo

20. Juan Marichal allowed the most home runs in Giants franchise history, with 315.

    a. True
    b. False

QUIZ ANSWERS

1. A – 646

2. B – False, Christy Mathewson

3. C – 12 times

4. D – Jeff Kent

5. B – Christy Mathewson

6. D – Mel Ott

7. B – False, John McGraw

8. A – Robb Nen

9. B – Mike Tiernan

10. D – Bill Terry

11. A – Barry Bonds

12. B – False, Willie Mays

13. D – Mickey Welch

14. C – George Davis

15. A – Barry Bonds

16. C – Bobby Bonds

17. A – True

18. D – Willie Mays

19. B – Rod Beck and Brian Wilson

20. A – True

DID YOU KNOW?

1. Christy Mathewson pitched the most innings in Giants franchise history, with 4,779.2. Second is Carl Hubbell, who pitched 3,590.1.

2. Bill Terry has the best career batting average in Giants franchise history, with an impressive .341. Mike Donlin is next best at .333.

3. Stan Javier holds the Giants franchise record for stolen base percentage, with 82.02%, and Mike Tiernan holds the franchise record for stolen bases, with 428. Good luck throwing them out!

4. Willie Mays has the most extra-base hits in Giants franchise history, with 1,289. Second on the list is Mel Ott, with 1,071.

5. Barry Bonds holds the Giants franchise record for at-bats per home run, with 10.7, meaning that he hit a home run in every 10.7 at-bats.

6. Matt Duffy holds the Giants' single-season record for stolen base percentage at 100%! In 2015, he was never thrown out while stealing a base.

7. Ron Hunt holds the Giants' single-season record for most times being hit by pitches. He was hit 26 times in 1970.

8. Christy Mathewson holds most of the Giants franchise pitching records. He comes in first in WAR, ERA, wins,

hits and walks per IP, innings pitched, strikeouts, games started, complete games, shutouts, hits, losses, batters faced, fielding-independent pitching, adjusted pitching runs, and adjusted pitching wins.

9. Mickey Welch holds the Giants' single-season record for wins, with 44 in 1885. Second on the list is Tim Keefe with 42 the following season.

10. Tim Keefe and Mickey Welch are tied for the Giants' single-season record for complete games, with a whopping 62 each. Welch threw 62 complete games in 1884, and Tim Keefe did it in 1886.

CHAPTER 7:

THE TRADE MARKET

QUIZ TIME!

1. In 1996, the Giants acquired _____ from the Anaheim Angels in exchange for pitchers Allen Watson and Fausto Macey.

   a. Jeff Kent

   b. J.T. Snow

   c. José Vizcaino

   d. Stan Javier

2. On deadline day in 2010, the Giants acquired pitcher _____ from the Pittsburgh Pirates in exchange for outfielder John Bowker and pitcher Joe Martinez.

   a. Santiago Casilla

   b. Javier Lopez

   c. Jeremy Affeldt

   d. Jonathan Sanchez

3. In December 2015, pitcher Jeff Samardzija signed with the Giants as a free agent.

a. True

b. False

4. In 1997, the Giants acquired pitcher Robb Nen from the _____ in exchange for pitchers Joe Fontenot, Mick Pageler, and Mike Villano.

   a. Cincinnati Reds
   b. Minnesota Twins
   c. Los Angeles Dodgers
   d. Florida Marlins

5. The Giants sent seven players and $300,000 to the Oakland A's in exchange for pitcher Vida Blue in 1978.

   a. True
   b. False

6. In 2012, the Giants traded shortstop Charlie Culberson to the Colorado Rockies in exchange for _____.

   a. Ryan Theriot
   b. Joaquin Arias
   c. Marco Scutaro
   d. Conor Gillaspie

7. In 2012, the Giants traded _____, Tommy Joseph, and Seth Rosin to the Philadelphia Phillies in exchange for Hunter Pence.

   a. Gregor Blanco
   b. Xavier Nady
   c. Eli Whiteside
   d. Nate Schierholtz

8. Which team traded Christy Mathewson to the Giants in 1900?

    a. Cincinnati Reds

    b. New York Highlanders

    c. Boston Americans

    d. Philadelphia Athletics

9. What year did the Giants sign Barry Bonds in free agency?

    a. 1990

    b. 1991

    c. 1992

    d. 1993

10. To acquire Jeff Kent in 1996, the Giants sent third baseman Matt Williams to the Cleveland Indians.

    a. True

    b. False

11. In 2011, the Giants traded _____ to the New York Mets in exchange for Carlos Beltran.

    a. R.A. Dickey

    b. Zack Wheeler

    c. Matt Harvey

    d. Jeurys Familia

12. The Giants have so far only made six trades with the Arizona Diamondbacks…ever.

    a. True

    b. False

13. How many trades have the Giants made with the Oakland A's all time (as of June 2020)?

    a. 3
    b. 9
    c. 12
    d. 15

14. The Giants have never made a trade with the Los Angeles Dodgers.

    a. True
    b. False

15. In 2015, Barry Bonds came out of retirement and signed with the Giants for one last season to redeem himself after his steroid scandal.

    a. True
    b. False

16. In 1966, the Giants traded _____ to the St. Louis Cardinals and received pitcher Ray Sadecki in return.

    a. Willie Mays
    b. Willie McCovey
    c. Jesus Alou
    d. Orlando Cepeda

17. In 2003, the Giants received catcher A.J. Pierzynski from the _____ in exchange for pitchers Joe Nathan, Francisco Liriano, and Boof Bonser.

    a. Kansas City Royals
    b. Chicago White Sox

c. Minnesota Twins

d. Texas Rangers

18. In 1971, the Giants traded pitcher Gaylord Perry to the

_____.

a. Atlanta Braves

b. Cleveland Indians

c. New York Yankees

d. Seattle Mariners

19. The Giants have made ___ trades with the Colorado Rockies in franchise history (as of June 2020).

a. 0

b. 4

c. 15

d. 24

20. The Giants acquired outfielder Angel Pagan from the New York Mets on December 7, 2011, in exchange for Ramon Ramirez and Andres Torres.

a. True

b. False

QUIZ ANSWERS

1. B – J.T. Snow

2. B – Javier Lopez

3. A – True

4. D – Florida Marlins

5. A – True

6. C – Marco Scutaro

7. D – Nate Schierholtz

8. A – Cincinnati Reds

9. C – 1992

10. A – True

11. B – Zack Wheeler

12. A – True

13. D – 15

14. B – False

15. B – False

16. D – Orlando Cepeda

17. C – Minnesota Twins

18. B – Cleveland Indians

19. B – 4

20. A – True

DID YOU KNOW?

1. The San Francisco Giants had the 12th largest payroll in Major League Baseball in 2019 at $138.3 million. The Boston Red Sox had the largest payroll at $213 million.

2. In 1974, the Giants traded Bobby Bonds to the New York Yankees for Bobby Murcer.

3. On October 25, 1973, the Giants traded Willie McCovey and Bernie Williams to the San Diego Padres for Mike Caldwell.

4. The Giants have only made six trades with the Toronto Blue Jays all time (as of June 2020).

5. Some consider the 2011 Miguel Tejada signing to be one of the worst signings the Giants have made in recent history. Although his career as a whole was impressive, his year spent with the Giants was subpar. He hit only .239 with 4 home runs and 26 RBI. The Giants released him near the end of the season...after having signed him to a $6.5 million contract.

6. Signing Barry Zito in free agency is another signing that is considered to be a bad move on the Giants' part. His curveball made him a dominant force across the bay in Oakland, but it didn't translate well to San Francisco. Other than a comeback season in 2012, Zito's time with the Giants was disappointing. They signed him to a 7-year,

$126 million contract, only for him to have an ERA above 4.00 each season he spent with them.

7. On January 15, 2018, the Giants traded Kyle Crick and Bryan Reynolds to the Pittsburgh Pirates for outfielder Andrew McCutchen. McCutchen played in 130 games for the Giants in 2018 but was traded in August to the New York Yankees.

8. On July 5, 1987, the Giants traded Chris Brown, Mark Grant, Mark Davis, and Keith Comstock to the San Diego Padres for Kevin Mitchell, Dave Dravecky, and Craig Lefferts.

9. On August 21, 1987, the Giants traded Jeff Robinson and Scott Medvin to the Pittsburgh Pirates for pitcher Rick Reuschel.

10. On November 7, 2011, the Giants acquired Melky Cabrera from the Kansas City Royals in exchange for Jonathan Sanchez and Ryan Verdugo.

CHAPTER 8:

DRAFT DAY

QUIZ TIME!

1. With the ___ overall pick in the 1st round of the 2006 MLB Draft, the San Francisco Giants selected pitcher Tim Lincecum.

    a. 1st
    b. 2nd
    c. 6th
    d. 10th

2. With the 10th overall pick in the 1st round of the 2007 MLB Draft, the San Francisco Giants selected _____.

    a. Buster Posey
    b. Madison Bumgarner
    c. Matt Cain
    d. Joe Panik

3. With the 5th overall pick in the 1st round of the 2008 MLB Draft, the San Francisco Giants selected catcher Buster Posey from _____.

a. University of Georgia

b. University of Florida

c. Notre Dame University

d. Florida State University

4. With the ___ overall pick in the 1st round of the 2011 MLB Draft, the San Francisco Giants selected shortstop Joe Panik.

a. 24th

b. 29th

c. 6th

d. 11th

5. With the 2nd overall pick in the 1st round of the 1985 MLB Draft, the San Francisco Giants selected first baseman Will Clark from _____.

a. University of Tennessee

b. University of Southern California

c. Mississippi State University

d. Vanderbilt University

6. Shortstop Brandon Crawford was drafted by the San Francisco Giants in the _____ round of the 2008 MLB Draft out of UCLA.

a. 2nd

b. 3rd

c. 4th

d. 5th

7. First baseman Brandon Belt was drafted in the 11th round of the 2006 MLB Draft by the Boston Red Sox. He was then drafted in the 11th round of the 2007 MLB Draft by the Atlanta Braves. Finally, he was drafted in the 5th round of the 2009 MLB Draft by the San Francisco Giants, the team he has been with ever since.

   a. True
   b. False

8. First baseman J.T. Snow was drafted in the 5th round of the 1989 MLB Draft by the _____.

   a. Chicago White Sox
   b. Baltimore Orioles
   c. New York Yankees
   d. Boston Red Sox

9. With the 3rd overall pick in the 1st round of the 1986 MLB Draft, the San Francisco Giants selected _____ from the University of Nevada-Las Vegas.

   a. Jason Grilli
   b. Matt White
   c. Terry Mulholland
   d. Matt Williams

10. In the 43rd round of the 2009 MLB Draft, the San Francisco Giants selected former San Francisco 49ers quarterback Colin Kaepernick.

   a. True
   b. False

11. Former Giants outfielder Angel Pagan was drafted by the New York Mets in the 4th round of the _____ MLB Draft out of Republica de Colombia High School in Puerto Rico.

   a. 1997
   b. 1998
   c. 1999
   d. 2000

12. Barry Bonds was drafted by the San Francisco Giants in the 2nd round of the 1982 MLB Draft out of high school. He was then drafted by the Pittsburgh Pirates in the 1st round (6th overall) in the 1985 MLB Draft.

   a. True
   b. False

13. With the 25th overall pick in the 1st round of the 2002 MLB Draft, the San Francisco Giants selected pitcher _____.

   a. Matt Cain
   b. Brian Wilson
   c. Travis Blackley
   d. Sergio Romo

14. With the 14th overall pick in the 1st round of the 1965 MLB Draft, the San Francisco Giants selected _____.

   a. Dave Rader
   b. Rob Dressler
   c. Bob Reynolds
   d. Al Gallagher

15. Former Giants manager Dusty Baker was drafted in the 26th round of the 1967 MLB Draft by the _____.

    a. Los Angeles Dodgers
    b. Oakland Athletics
    c. Atlanta Braves
    d. San Francisco Giants

16. The current Giants manager, outfielder Gabe Kapler, was drafted in the 57th round of the 1995 MLB Draft by the

    _____.

    a. Detroit Tigers
    b. Colorado Rockies
    c. Tampa Bay Rays
    d. Texas Rangers

17. Giants outfielder Hunter Pence was drafted in the 2nd round of the 2004 MLB Draft by the _____.

    a. Texas Rangers
    b. Houston Astros
    c. Philadelphia Phillies
    d. Montreal Expos

18. What college was pitcher Madison Bumgarner drafted out of?

    a. University of North Carolina
    b. North Carolina State University
    c. Duke University
    d. He did not attend college; he was drafted out of high school.

19. Former Giants manager Bruce Bochy's son, Brett Bochy, was drafted by the San Francisco Giants in the _____ round of the 2010 MLB Draft out of the University of Kansas.

   a. 2nd
   b. 10th
   c. 20th
   d. 21st

20. In the 1st round of the 1959 MLB Draft, the San Francisco Giants selected first baseman Willie McCovey.

   a. True
   b. False

QUIZ ANSWERS

1. D – 10th

2. B – Madison Bumgarner

3. D – Florida State University

4. B – 29th

5. C – Mississippi State University

6. C – 4th

7. A – True

8. C – New York Yankees

9. D – Matt Williams

10. B – False, Chicago Cubs

11. C – 1999

12. A – True

13. A – Matt Cain

14. D – Al Gallagher

15. C – Atlanta Braves

16. A – Detroit Tigers

17. B – Houston Astros

18. D – He did not attend college; he was drafted out of high school.

19. C – 20th

20. B – False, The draft did not exist until 1965.

DID YOU KNOW?

1. The Giants drafted centerfielder Hunter Bishop out of Arizona State University with their 1st round pick in the 2019 MLB Draft. In 2019, they chose 11 players out of high school and 29 out of college.

2. In 2010, the Giants secured their first World Series win since moving to San Francisco. That same year, their 1st round draft choice was centerfielder Gary Brown out of Cal State-Fullerton. He made his debut with the Giants but played for them for only a short period in 2014. The Los Angeles Angels picked him up off waivers in 2015 but released him a year later. He is no longer in Major League Baseball.

3. The Giants drafted pitcher Sergio Romo in the 28th round of the 2005 MLB Draft out of Colorado Mesa University.

4. Former Giants closer Brian Wilson was drafted by the Cleveland Indians in the 30th round of the 2000 MLB Draft out of high school. He was then drafted by the Giants in the 24th round of the 2003 MLB Draft out of Louisiana State University.

5. Former Giants pitcher Jeremy Affeldt was drafted by the Kansas City Royals in the 3rd round of the 1997 MLB Draft out of high school.

6. Giants pitcher Jeff Samardzija was drafted by the Chicago

Cubs in the 5th round of the 2006 MLB Draft out of the University of Notre Dame. He was a star football player at Notre Dame and was recognized as a two-time All-American wide receiver.

7. Former Giant Mike Morse was drafted by the Chicago White Sox in the 3rd round of the 2000 MLB Draft out of high school.

8. The Chicago Cubs drafted infielder Ryan Theriot in the 3rd round of the 2001 MLB Draft out of Louisiana State University. He played eight years in the MLB with the Cubs, Dodgers, Cardinals, and Giants.

9. Tim Lincecum was drafted by the Cubs in the 48th round of the 2003 MLB Draft, but he did not sign with them so he could attend college. He was drafted twice more, by the Cleveland Indians and then San Francisco Giants, who did sign him.

10. Former Giants rightfielder Nate Schierholtz was drafted by the San Francisco Giants in the 2nd round of the 2003 MLB Draft out of Chabot College in Hayward, CA.

CHAPTER 9:

ODDS & ENDS

QUIZ TIME!

1. Former Giants second baseman Jeff Kent was a contestant on which TV reality show?

    a. *The Bachelor*
    b. *Big Brother*
    c. *Dancing with the Stars*
    d. *Survivor*

2. Madison Bumgarner once dated a girl named Madison Bumgarner.

    a. True
    b. False

3. What is Buster Posey's favorite show to watch with his wife Kristin?

    a. *The Real Housewives of Atlanta*
    b. *The Bachelorette*
    c. *Ghost Adventures*
    d. *Hell's Kitchen*

4. Brandon Belt and Barry Zito presented the American Country Music Award for Artist of the Year in 2012 to _____.

   a. Maren Morris
   b. Blake Shelton
   c. Carrie Underwood
   d. Thomas Rhett

5. Tim Lincecum used to live in a tower where the main character from _____ lived in the book/movie.

   a. *Fifty Shades of Grey*
   b. *The Notebook*
   c. *The Hunger Games*
   d. *Harry Potter*

6. San Francisco outfielder Mike Yastrzemski is the _____ of MLB legend, Hall-of-Famer, and Triple Crown winner, Carl Yastrzemski.

   a. Cousin
   b. Son
   c. Nephew
   d. Grandson

7. Former Giants manager Bruce Bochy wrote a book in 2015 called *A Book of Walks* that highlights his love for walking around San Francisco and the cities he visited as an MLB manager.

   a. True
   b. False

8. Brett Bochy was managed by his _____, Bruce Bochy, when he played for the Giants in 2014-15.

    a. Cousin
    b. Dad
    c. Uncle
    d. Grandpa

9. Which former Giants player gave Pablo Sandoval his nickname, "Kung Fu Panda"?

    a. Buster Posey
    b. Madison Bumgarner
    c. Barry Zito
    d. Brandon Belt

10. The Giants hold an annual _____ night because the company is based in the Bay Area.

    a. Apple
    b. Levi Strauss
    c. Twitter
    d. Pixar

11. Hunter Pence rides a _____ to Oracle Park. It was once stolen outside of a restaurant.

    a. Bike
    b. Scooter
    c. Vespa
    d. Skateboard

12. Madison Bumgarner was raised in Bumtown, North Carolina.

a. True

b. False

13. When Stephen Vogt was with the Oakland A's, he did a popular impersonation of which popular *Saturday Night Live* sketch character?

    a. MacGruber

    b. Matt Foley (Van Down by the River Guy)

    c. Stefon

    d. Church Lady

14. Which member of the 2010 Giants World Series championship team is now an analyst for MLB Network?

    a. Mark DeRosa

    b. Tim Lincecum

    c. Aubrey Huff

    d. Cody Ross

15. Which former Giants pitcher was the first Cy Young Award winner to appear on the *Billboard* music charts?

    a. Tim Lincecum

    b. Mike McCormick

    c. Tim Hudson

    d. Barry Zito

16. After retirement, former Giants pitcher Tim Hudson went back to college at Auburn University to obtain his degree.

    a. True

    b. False

17. Which former Giants pitcher is legally blind without corrective lenses?

    a. Tim Lincecum
    b. Sergio Romo
    c. Jeremy Affeldt
    d. Jake Peavy

18. In which city does the Giants' Double-A farm team play?

    a. Sacramento, California
    b. Indianapolis, Indiana
    c. Richmond, Virginia
    d. San Jose, California

19. Which pitcher threw the first perfect game in franchise history?

    a. Matt Cain
    b. Tim Lincecum
    c. Madison Bumgarner
    d. Jeff Samardzija

20. During their visit to the White House after winning the 2014 World Series, the Giants presented President Barack Obama with a Giants jersey that included his name and number 44 because he was the 44th president of the United States.

    a. True
    b. False

QUIZ ANSWERS

1. D – *Survivor*

2. A – True

3. B – *The Bachelorette*

4. C – Carrie Underwood

5. A – *Fifty Shades of Grey*

6. D – Grandson

7. A – True

8. B – Dad

9. C – Barry Zito

10. D – Pixar

11. B – Scooter

12. A – True

13. B – Matt Foley (Van Down by the River Guy)

14. A – Mark DeRosa

15. D – Barry Zito

16. A – True

17. D – Jake Peavy

18. C – Richmond, Virginia (The Flying Squirrels)

19. A – Matt Cain

20. A – True

DID YOU KNOW?

1. During the 2002 World Series, Dusty Baker's son (then a toddler) was a Giants' batboy. Kenny Lofton hit a triple, and J.T. Snow rounded third on his way home. Dusty's son, Darren, then ran to home plate to collect Lofton's bat. Somehow, Snow reacted quickly enough to grab Darren by the jacket to save him from being trampled by Giants…literally. It is one of the most famous odd moments in World Series history. Darren is now a college baseball player at Cal-Berkeley.

2. When Brandon Crawford was 5 years old, the Giants were very close to leaving the Bay Area to move to Florida. As a devastated Bay Area resident, Crawford was photographed at Candlestick Park by a *San Francisco Chronicle* photographer. Of course, the Giants didn't move to Florida, but they did move to Oracle Park when Crawford was in middle school. When the team moved, the Crawford family bought a brick on Willie Mays Plaza. He has played for his favorite baseball team since 2011.

3. September 20, 2015 was *Full House* Night at Oracle Park. Jodie Sweetin, who played Stephanie, announced "Play Ball!" and the show's creator, Jeff Franklin, threw out the first pitch. Each fan in attendance got a "Full Clubhouse" snow globe giveaway.

4. The Giants have the longest Home Run Derby drought in

the National League. The last Giant to participate in a Home Run Derby was Barry Bonds....Kinda wish Madison Bumgarner would participate, don't you?

5. Former Giants manager Felipe Alou also managed the Montreal Expos. He is a huge advocate for getting a team back in Montreal. He is quoted as saying: "Baseball will be back to Montreal. I want to see it. I want it to happen before I die. I will see it."

6. Gabe Kapler is only the seventh Jewish manager in MLB history. He also went to the same high school as Ice Cube. Those facts don't really have anything to do with one another, but whatever.

7. Pitcher Derek Holland was once kicked out of a Counting Crows concert in New Jersey while visiting to play the New York Yankees.

8. Madison Bumgarner has a secret rodeo identity. He competes in rodeo and roping competitions under the alias "Mason Saunders."

9. Madison Bumgarner got married in denim jeans and carried a pocketknife with him on his wedding day.

10. Hunter Pence's wife Lexi has a YouTube channel that often features content with her and Hunter. The channel is called "Let's Get Lexi."

CHAPTER 10:

OUTFIELDERS

QUIZ TIME!

1. Which team did former Giants outfielder Cody Ross NOT play for during his career?

    a. Oakland A's
    b. Los Angeles Dodgers
    c. Tampa Bay Rays
    d. Arizona Diamondbacks

2. Moises Alou did not like to wear batting gloves. Instead, he peed on his hands to make them tougher.

    a. True
    b. False

3. In what year was former Giant Orlando Cepeda elected to the National Baseball Hall of Fame?

    a. 1999
    b. 1995
    c. 1993
    d. 1990

4. Former Giants outfielder Mike Morse never hit a home run in his one season spent on the team in 2014.

   a. True
   b. False

5. Which of these teams has former MLB outfielder and former Giants manager Dusty Baker NOT managed (as of the 2019 season) in his coaching career?

   a. Chicago Cubs
   b. Washington Nationals
   c. Cincinnati Reds
   d. Texas Rangers

6. How many games did outfielder Nate Schierholtz play in his 2010 season with the Giants?

   a. 80
   b. 108
   c. 162
   d. 137

7. Angel Pagan played his entire 11-year career with the Giants.

   a. True
   b. False

8. How many seasons did Barry Bonds play for the Giants?

   a. 5
   b. 12
   c. 20
   d. 15

9. Which team has former Giants outfielder Andrew McCutchen NOT played for so far in his career (as of the 2019 season)?

   a. Pittsburgh Pirates
   b. New York Yankees
   c. Milwaukee Brewers
   d. Philadelphia Phillies

10. How many seasons did centerfielder Kenny Lofton play for the Giants?

   a. 1
   b. 2
   c. 3
   d. 4

11. Which former Giants outfielder is currently manager of the Los Angeles Dodgers?

   a. Andres Torres
   b. Nate Schierholtz
   c. Dave Roberts
   d. Cody Ross

12. Hunter Pence played in all 162 games for the Giants in 2013 AND 2014.

   a. True
   b. False

13. How many home runs did centerfielder Austin Jackson hit as a member of the Giants during the 2018 season?

a. 0

b. 5

c. 10

d. 15

14. Which former Giants outfielder was named the 2013 Wilson NL Defensive Player of the Year?

a. Cole Gillespie

b. Andres Torres

c. Angel Pagan

d. Gregor Blanco

15. What was Giants outfielder Hunter Pence's season batting average in 2017?

a. .277

b. .260

c. .286

d. .236

16. Denard Span hit 5 triples in 32 games with the Giants in 2016.

a. True

b. False

17. How many games did Tyler Colvin play in for the Giants during the 2014 season?

a. 12

b. 44

c. 57

d. 156

18. Angel Pagan hit the most triples in the National League, with 15, in which year?

   a. 2016
   b. 2015
   c. 2014
   d. 2012

19. How many MLB All-Star Games did former Giants outfielder Carlos Beltran play in during his career?

   a. 3
   b. 6
   c. 9
   d. 12

20. Former Giants outfielder Marlon Byrd played for 10 different MLB teams during his career.

   a. True
   b. False

QUIZ ANSWERS

1. C – Tampa Bay Rays

2. A – True

3. A – 1999

4. B – False, He hit 16.

5. D – Texas Rangers

6. D – 137

7. B – False, He played with the Cubs, Mets, and Giants.

8. D – 15

9. C – Milwaukee Brewers

10. A – 1

11. C – Dave Roberts

12. A – True

13. A – 0

14. D – Gregor Blanco

15. B – .260

16. A – True

17. C – 57

18. D – 2012

19. C – 9

20. A – True

DID YOU KNOW?

1. Pedro Feliz played in 874 games in his eight seasons with the San Francisco Giants.

2. After his retirement, Darryl Hamilton became an analyst for MLB Network. In 2015, he died in an apparent murder-suicide, in which his girlfriend ended his life and her own.

3. Although Cody Ross and David Ross have the same last name, played baseball, are bald, and have facial hair, they are in no way related.

4. Former Giants outfielder Nate Schierholtz is now an operating partner for KLV Capital, and he has an Arizona real estate license.

5. Former Giants outfielder Deion Sanders also played in the NFL. This means he played for both the San Francisco Giants and the San Francisco 49ers.

6. Former Giants outfielder Darryl Strawberry was in the iconic episode of *The Simpsons*, "Homer at the Bat," in season 3. The episode also featured Mike Scioscia, Roger Clemens, Ken Griffey Jr., Ozzie Smith, Jose Canseco, Roger Clemens, Steve Sax, and Don Mattingly. All the players voiced themselves.

7. Former Giants outfielder Chili Davis has spent his retirement from baseball as a hitting coach for the Oakland A's, Boston Red Sox, Chicago Cubs, and New York Mets.

8. Former Giants outfielder Mike Aldrete is the Oakland A's current first base coach.

9. Dave Henderson is known for his time with the Oakland A's, but he actually played one season for the Giants before he made his way across the bay.

10. Dusty Baker is known for being one of the best Giants managers of all time, but he also played one season for the Giants during his playing career, back in 1984. He also played for both of the Giants' biggest rivals, the Dodgers and the A's.

CHAPTER 11:

INFIELDERS

QUIZ TIME!

1. How many home runs did Giants shortstop Brandon Crawford hit during the 2015 season?

    a. 18

    b. 19

    c. 21

    d. 27

2. In 2009, Juan Uribe won an NL Defensive Player of the Year Award.

    a. True

    b. False

3. After retirement, which former Giants infielder took a position as a studio analyst for MLB Network and became the broadcast announcer in the video game *MLB: The Show*?

    a. Conor Gillaspie

    b. Orlando Cabrera

   c. Mark DeRosa

   d. Ryan Theriot

4. How many games did Brandon Belt play in for the Giants in 2012?

   a. 145

   b. 150

   c. 160

   d. 100

5. For which team did Pablo Sandoval play in between his two stints with the Giants?

   a. Miami Marlins

   b. Kansas City Royals

   c. Texas Rangers

   d. Boston Red Sox

6. How many seasons did Omar Vizquel play in the Major Leagues?

   a. 16

   b. 24

   c. 20

   d. 28

7. J.T. Snow played his entire MLB career with the Giants.

   a. True

   b. False

8. Which former Giants infielder was named to the National Baseball Hall of Fame in 1990?

a. Orlando Cepeda

b. Tony Lazzeri

c. Joe Morgan

d. Red Schoendienst

9. Which MLB team did former Giants infielder Steve Scarsone NOT play for during his baseball career?

a. St. Louis Cardinals

b. Baltimore Orioles

c. Kansas City Royals

d. Houston Astros

10. How many home runs did third baseman Matt Williams hit in his 10 seasons with the Giants?

a. 247

b. 223

c. 259

d. 270

11. How many hits did former Giants first baseman Will Clark accumulate during the 1989 season?

a. 125

b. 201

c. 196

d. 175

12. Kevin Mitchell led the Giants in home runs during the 1988 season.

a. True

b. False

13. Current Giants TV announcer Duane Kuiper played second base for the Giants for _____ seasons.

    a. 2
    b. 4
    c. 6
    d. 8

14. Current Giants announcer Duane Kuiper played for two teams during his MLB playing career; the Giants and the

    _____.

    a. Milwaukee Brewers
    b. Toronto Blue Jays
    c. Philadelphia Phillies
    d. Cleveland Indians

15. How many seasons did Willie McCovey play for the San Francisco Giants?

    a. 12
    b. 19
    c. 23
    d. 15

16. Marco Scutaro was never named to an MLB All-Star Game during his career.

    a. True
    b. False

17. Which infielder did NOT play for BOTH the Giants AND the Los Angeles Dodgers during his MLB career?

a. Jeff Kent

b. Ryan Theriot

c. Juan Uribe

d. Will Clark

18. Which infielder did NOT play for BOTH the Giants AND the Oakland A's during his MLB career?

a. Jim Davenport

b. Marco Scutaro

c. Miguel Tejada

d. Tito Fuentes

19. Joe Panik was named to the MLB All-Star Game in _____.

a. 2015

b. 2016

c. 2017

d. 2018

20. Giants third baseman Evan Longoria was named the American League Rookie of the Year in 2008.

a. True

b. False

QUIZ ANSWERS

1. C – 21

2. B – False, He did in 2013 and 2014 with the Dodgers.

3. C – Mark DeRosa

4. A – 145

5. D – Boston Red Sox

6. B – 24

7. B – False, He also played for the Yankees, Angels, and Red Sox.

8. C – Joe Morgan

9. D – Houston Astros

10. A – 247

11. C – 196

12. B – False, Will Clark

13. B – 4

14. D – Cleveland Indians

15. B – 19

16. B – False, He was named in 2013.

17. D – Will Clark

18. A – Jim Davenport

19. A – 2015

20. A – True

DID YOU KNOW?

1. Giants first baseman Brandon Belt was named the National League Player of the Week on August 11, 2013, and May 20, 2018.

2. Evan Longoria has played for only two MLB teams so far in his career. The Tampa Bay Rays and, of course, the Giants.

3. As of the end of the 2019 season, shortstop Brandon Crawford has appeared in two MLB All-Star Games, won a Silver Slugger in 2015, and has also won three Gold Gloves.

4. Pablo Sandoval won the 2012 National League Babe Ruth Award, which is given annually to the player who had the best postseason performance.

5. Second baseman Joe Panik won a National League Gold Glove Award in 2016.

6. The Giants drafted infielder Kelby Tomlinson in the 12th round of the 2011 MLB Draft.

7. Infielder Joaquin Arias played for the Giants, New York Mets, and Texas Rangers during his career. Before retirement, he was signed by the New York Yankees as a free agent, but he never played for them.

8. Former New York Giants manager and MLB infielder Cap

Anson has the highest WAR (wins above replacement) in Cubs franchise history at a whopping 85.8.

9. Former Giant Casey McGehee was named the 2014 NL Comeback Player of the Year.

10. Marco Scutaro led the NL in singles in 2012, with 147.

CHAPTER 12:

PITCHERS & CATCHERS

QUIZ TIME!

1. Which pitcher has NOT pitched for both the Giants and Oakland A's in his MLB career?

   a. Vida Blue
   b. Santiago Casilla
   c. Matt Cain
   d. Barry Zito

2. Current Oakland A's manager Bob Melvin played for the Giants as a catcher for three seasons.

   a. True
   b. False

3. Which pitcher has NOT pitched for both the Giants and Los Angeles Dodgers in his MLB career?

   a. Juan Marichal
   b. Tim Lincecum
   c. Brad Penny
   d. Brian Wilson

4. Which former Giants manager was a catcher in his playing career?

   a. Dusty Baker
   b. Felipe Alou
   c. Bruce Bochy
   d. Frank Robinson

5. As of the end of the 2019 season, how many MLB All-Star Games has Buster Posey been named to?

   a. 4
   b. 5
   c. 6
   d. 7

6. How many saves did Sergio Romo record for the Giants during the 2013 season?

   a. 38
   b. 14
   c. 23
   d. 43

7. Tim Lincecum was named to four MLB All-Star Games in his career.

   a. True
   b. False

8. Juan Marichal was named to ___ MLB All-Star Games during his career.

   a. 8
   b. 9

c. 10

d. 11

9. How many games did catcher A.J. Pierzynski play for the Giants during the 2004 season?

   a. 80

   b. 100

   c. 112

   d. 131

10. What was Madison Bumgarner's win-loss record for the 2014 season?

   a. 18-10

   b. 18-9

   c. 15-9

   d. 15-10

11. On June 13, 2012, Matt Cain threw the _____ perfect game in MLB history.

   a. 19th

   b. 22nd

   c. 24th

   d. 27th

12. Bruce Bochy played for the Giants during his MLB career as a catcher.

   a. True

   b. False

13. How many saves did Brian Wilson accumulate for the Giants during the 2010 season?

a. 46

b. 77

c. 11

d. 38

14. How many saves has Madison Bumgarner accumulated so far in his career (as of the 2019 season)?

    a. 4

    b. 2

    c. 1

    d. 0

15. Ryan Vogelsong pitched for two MLB teams during his 12-year career, the Giants and the _____.

    a. Pittsburgh Pirates

    b. Texas Rangers

    c. Los Angeles Angels of Anaheim

    d. Colorado Rockies

16. Former Giants catcher Steven Vogt got his nickname "I Believe" from Oakland A's bleacher fans.

    a. True

    b. False

17. How many complete games did Tim Hudson throw for the Giants in 2014?

    a. 0

    b. 1

    c. 2

    d. 3

18. How many intentional walks did former Giants pitcher Jeremy Affeldt throw during the 2013 season?

    a. 0
    b. 2
    c. 4
    d. 5

19. How many home runs did Madison Bumgarner hit in 2015?

    a. 2
    b. 3
    c. 4
    d. 5

20. In Barry Zito's seven seasons spent with the Giants, he only had a winning pitching record for one of those seasons.

    a. True
    b. False

QUIZ ANSWERS

1. C – Matt Cain

2. A – True

3. B – Tim Lincecum

4. C – Bruce Bochy

5. C – 6

6. A – 38

7. A – True

8. C – 10

9. D – 131

10. A – 18-10

11. B – 22nd

12. B – False, He was a catcher for the Houston Astros, New York Mets, and San Diego Padres.

13. D – 38

14. D – 0

15. A – Pittsburgh Pirates

16. A – True

17. B – 1

18. D – 5

19. D – 5

20. A – True

DID YOU KNOW?

1. On May 25, 2011, Buster Posey was injured in a collision at home plate with Scott Cousins of the Florida Marlins. He suffered a fractured fibula and torn ligaments in his ankle, which required season-ending surgery.

2. Before Buster Posey made his MLB debut, Bengie Molina was the Giants' starting catcher. Bengie is one of three brothers who have won World Series rings as catchers. The other two brothers are José and Yadier.

3. Matt Cain pitched his entire 13-year MLB career with the Giants.

4. Current Giants TV announcer Mike Krukow pitched for the Giants from 1983 to 1989. He also played for the Chicago Cubs and Philadelphia Phillies.

5. Hall of Fame pitcher Goose Gossage pitched for the Giants in 1989. He also played for the A's, Yankees, White Sox, Pirates, Padres, Rangers, Cubs, and Mariners during his 22-season career.

6. Vida Blue was named the 1978 NL Pitcher of the Year by *The Sporting News*. That season, his win-loss record with the Giants was 18-10.

7. Gaylord Perry won 23 games for the Giants in 1970. He started 41 games that season, pitched 328.2 innings, and faced 1,336 batters.

8. Juan Marichal won 26 games for the Giants in 1968. He threw 30 complete games that season and faced 1,307 batters.

9. Pat Venditte, the first "switch-pitcher" (ambidextrous pitcher) in the Major Leagues, played for the Giants in 2019.

10. Juan Marichal gave up the most home runs in Giants franchise history, with 315. Second on the list is Carl Hubbell with 227 home runs given up.

CHAPTER 13:

EVERY OTHER YEAR

QUIZ TIME!

1. How many World Series have the Giants won in franchise history?

    a. 3

    b. 5

    c. 8

    d. 9

2. What kind of natural disaster interrupted the 1989 Bay Bridge World Series between the Giants and the Oakland A's?

    a. Earthquake

    b. Tornado

    c. Tsunami

    d. Hurricane

3. Which player was named World Series MVP in 2012?

    a. Buster Posey

    b. Madison Bumgarner

c. Pablo Sandoval

d. Brandon Crawford

4. What team did the Giants defeat in the 2010 World Series?

a. New York Yankees

b. Minnesota Twins

c. Detroit Tigers

d. Texas Rangers

5. What team did the Giants defeat in the 2014 World Series?

a. Texas Rangers

b. Kansas City Royals

c. Detroit Tigers

d. Seattle Mariners

6. How many games did the 2012 World Series go?

a. 4

b. 5

c. 6

d. 7

7. The Oakland A's swept the Giants in the 1989 World Series.

a. True

b. False

8. Who was the New York Giants' manager when they won the World Series in 1933?

a. Alvin Dark

b. Mel Ott

c. Bill Terry

d. Felipe Alou

9. Who was manager during all three of the San Francisco Giants' World Series wins? (2010, 2012, 2014)

a. Felipe Alou

b. Bruce Bochy

c. Dusty Baker

d. Frank Robinson

10. What team did the Giants defeat in the 1921 AND 1922 World Series?

a. Chicago White Sox

b. Washington Senators

c. New York Yankees

d. St. Louis Browns

11. What team did the Giants defeat in the 1954 World Series?

a. Baltimore Orioles

b. New York Yankees

c. Boston Red Sox

d. Cleveland Indians

12. The Giants have played in 20 World Series, which is a National League record.

a. True

b. False

13. Who was named the 2010 World Series MVP?

a. Buster Posey

b. Brandon Belt

c. Edgar Renteria

d. Matt Cain

14. Who was named the 2014 World Series MVP?

    a. Madison Bumgarner

    b. Hunter Pence

    c. Ryan Vogelsong

    d. Marco Scutaro

15. What year did the Giants win the World Series for the first time in franchise history?

    a. 1908

    b. 1921

    c. 1905

    d. 1901

16. The San Francisco Giants have never won a World Series at home. They have always celebrated their championship at the opposing team's stadium.

    a. True

    b. False

17. Who was the Giants' starting pitcher for Game 5 of the 2010 World Series?

    a. Madison Bumgarner

    b. Tim Lincecum

    c. Matt Cain

    d. Ryan Vogelsong

18. What was the final score of Game 2 of the 2014 World Series?

a. Giants 7, Royals 2

b. Giants 4, Royals 1

c. Royals 7, Giants 2

d. Royals 4, Giants 1

19. Which Giants player did NOT have a hit in Game 4 of the 2012 World Series?

a. Buster Posey

b. Gregor Blanco

c. Brandon Crawford

d. Angel Pagan

20. Catcher Buster Posey won the National League Rookie of the Year Award and a World Series championship the same year.

a. True

b. False

QUIZ ANSWERS

1. C – 8

2. A – Earthquake

3. C – Pablo Sandoval

4. D – Texas Rangers

5. B – Kansas City Royals

6. A – 4

7. A – True

8. C – Bill Terry

9. B – Bruce Bochy

10. C – New York Yankees

11. D – Cleveland Indians

12. A – True

13. C – Edgar Renteria

14. A – Madison Bumgarner

15. C – 1905

16. A – True

17. B – Tim Lincecum

18. C – Royals 7, Giants 2

19. D – Angel Pagan

20. A – True, 2010

DID YOU KNOW?

1. The Loma Prieta Earthquake interrupted the A's/Giants World Series in 1989. The series was delayed while the bay healed. The A's ended up sweeping the Giants four games to none.

2. The World Series MVP trophy is a wooden pedestal topped with a bronze sculpture of Giants legend, Willie Mays. It is now called the Willie Mays World Series MVP Award.

3. The Giants won the World Series every other year from 2010 through 2014. If the pattern had persisted, they would have won in 2016, but the Chicago Cubs won the World Series that year, their first in 108 years.

4. Some Giants won all three rings since they were won in such close succession. Those players include Buster Posey, Jeremy Affeldt, Madison Bumgarner, Matt Cain, Santiago Casilla, Tim Lincecum, Javier Lopez, Sergio Romo, and Pablo Sandoval.

5. The Giants have won eight World Series in franchise history: 1905, 1921, 1922, 1933, 1954, 2010, 2012, and 2014. They won their last championship in New York in 1954, four years before moving to California.

6. Tim Lincecum got the World Series Game 1 start in 2010, Barry Zito got the Game 1 start in 2012, and Madison Bumgarner got the Game 1 start in 2014.

7. The 1954 World Series MVP was outfielder Jim "Dusty" Rhodes. His career was pretty underwhelming as a whole, but he had a starring role for the Giants in the 1954 Fall Classic.

8. The Giants defeated the Washington Senators in the 1933 World Series in five games. This was the last World Series played in Washington, DC, until 2019, when the Washington Nationals took home the championship.

9. The 1921 World Series was the Yankees' first appearance ever in a World Series. They have been in 39 more since then. That was the last World Series to use a best-of-nine format.

10. All of the games in both the 1921 and 1922 World Series were played at the Polo Grounds because it was the home stadium for BOTH teams. The Yankees moved to Yankee Stadium in 1923.

CHAPTER 14:

HEATED RIVALRIES

QUIZ TIME!

1. Which team is not a Giants NL West rival?

   a. San Diego Padres

   b. Los Angeles Dodgers

   c. Seattle Mariners

   d. Arizona Diamondbacks

2. The Giants and Dodgers have never met in the MLB postseason.

   a. True

   b. False

3. In 2019, the Dodgers and Giants played their _____ game against each other, becoming only the third set of teams in the four major North American sports to do so.

   a. 1,995th

   b. 2,500th

   c. 2,000th

   d. 3,000th

4. The Los Angeles Dodgers have won the National League West 17 times, and the San Francisco Giants have won the National League West _____ times.

   a. 12
   b. 16
   c. 8
   d. 6

5. When the Giants play a series against their rival from across the bay, the Oakland A's, the series is called the

   _____.

   a. Bay Area Series
   b. Bay Bridge Series
   c. Golden Gate Bridge Series
   d. Pacific Ocean Series

6. The Giants have eight World Championships as of the end of the 2019 season. How many do the Dodgers have?

   a. 8
   b. 5
   c. 10
   d. 6

7. The A's and Giants shared Candlestick Park for a short period, which is a big part of their rivalry.

   a. True
   b. False

8. On May 11, 1963, which Dodgers pitcher threw a no-hitter against the Giants?

a. Larry Sherry

b. Bob Miller

c. Don Drysdale

d. Sandy Koufax

9. The Giants have eight World Series championships as of the end of the 2019 season. How many do the A's have?

a. 9

b. 10

c. 11

d. 12

10. How many games did the 1989 World Series between the Giants and A's go?

a. 4

b. 5

c. 6

d. 7

11. The current Oakland A's manager, _____, played as a catcher for the Giants from 1986-1988.

a. Bob Geren

b. Bob Melvin

c. Ken Macha

d. Art Howe

12. According to Tommy Lasorda, Jackie Robinson decided to retire rather than play for the Giants when he was traded to them in 1956. After 10 years with the Dodgers, he had come to hate the Giants and refused to play for them.

a. True

b. False

13. On March 31, 2011, Giants fan _____ was critically injured when fighting with two Dodgers fans in the Dodger Stadium parking lot.

    a. Bruce Snow

    b. Bruce Stow

    c. Bryan Snow

    d. Bryan Stow

14. Which player has NOT played for both the Dodgers and the Giants?

    a. Brian Wilson

    b. Jeff Kent

    c. J.T. Snow

    d. Juan Marichal

15. Which player has NOT played for both the A's and the Giants?

    a. Barry Zito

    b. Willie McCovey

    c. Andrew McCutchen

    d. Vida Blue

16. When the A's play the Giants, fans call it the "Battle of the Bay."

    a. True

    b. False

17. The Giants have won eight World Series championships as of the end of the 2019 season. How many have the Yankees won?

    a. 30
    b. 10
    c. 15
    d. 27

18. What is the current regular-season record between the Giants and A's (as of the end of the 2019 season)?

    a. 64 A's, 60 Giants
    b. 64 Giants, 60 A's
    c. 75 A's, 71 Giants
    d. 75 Giants, 71 A's

19. When was the first meeting between the Giants and the Dodgers? (The Giants were the New York Giants, and the Dodgers were the Brooklyn Bridegrooms.)

    a. May 30, 1888
    b. May 30, 1890
    c. May 3, 1890
    d. May 3, 1888

20. Since 2018, the Bay Bridge Series between the A's and Giants has had a trophy fashioned from a piece of the old Bay Bridge that collapsed during the 1989 World Series, in which the two teams faced each other. As of the 2019 season, each team has won the trophy once.

    a. True
    b. False

QUIZ ANSWERS

1. C – Seattle Mariners

2. A – True

3. B – 2,500th

4. C – 8

5. B – Bay Bridge Series

6. D – 6

7. B – False

8. D – Sandy Koufax

9. A – 9

10. A – 4 (The A's swept the Giants.)

11. B – Bob Melvin

12. A – True

13. D – Bryan Stow

14. C – J.T. Snow

15. C – Andrew McCutchen

16. A – True

17. D – 27

18. A – 64 A's, 60 Giants

19. C – May 3, 1890

20. A – True

DID YOU KNOW?

1. The A's and Giants did not meet in the regular season until June of 1997, when interleague play began, despite the fact that the A's moved out to the Bay Area in 1968.

2. The A's and Giants have met in four World Series. The Giants won in 1905, and the A's won in 1911, 1913, and 1989.

3. The Giants-Dodgers rivalry began in the late 1800s because, at that time, both teams were based in New York. The Yankees were a rival of both teams as well because of their location.

4. The Dodgers and Giants are currently tied for most National League Pennants, with 23 each.

5. After the Giants left for the West, New York got a new team, the Mets. The Mets inherited the colors of the Giants-Dodgers rivalry. That's why their colors are orange (Giants) and blue (Dodgers).

6. "The Big Three" was a group of three dominant A's pitchers in the early 2000s that consisted of Barry Zito, Tim Hudson, and Mark Mulder. Two of those three pitchers, Zito and Hudson, went on to play for the Giants.

7. The Giants and Yankees have met in the World Series seven times. The Giants won in 1921 and 1922, but the Yankees won all the World Series after that, in 1923, 1936, 1937, 1951, and 1962.

8. The Giants and Yankees briefly shared Hilltop Park in New York, which was a big part of their rivalry.

9. The Giants used to play in the "Subway Series" against the Yankees. The last Subway Series that the Giants participated in was in 1951.

10. The rivalry between the Giants and Dodgers is regarded as one of the most competitive rivalries in baseball. Some call it the greatest sports rivalry of all time. Yes, even over the Yankees and Red Sox.

CHAPTER 15:

THE AWARDS SECTION

QUIZ TIME!

1. Which Giants player won the NL MVP and an NL Silver Slugger Award in 2012?

    a. Marco Scutaro

    b. Pablo Sandoval

    c. Buster Posey

    d. Melky Cabrera

2. No Giants manager has ever won the National League Manager of the Year Award.

    a. True

    b. False

3. Who was the first Giants pitcher to win the Cy Young Award?

    a. Tim Lincecum

    b. Madison Bumgarner

    c. Juan Marichal

    d. Mike McCormick

4. Which Giant most recently won the NL Rookie of the Year Award?

   a. Robby Thompson
   b. Buster Posey
   c. Willie McCovey
   d. Orlando Cepeda

5. How many Gold Glove Awards has Brandon Crawford won so far in his career (as of the end of the 2019 season)?

   a. 3
   b. 2
   c. 6
   d. 1

6. Which Giant won the 2006 Willie Mac Award?

   a. Bengie Molina
   b. Mike Matheny
   c. Omar Vizquel
   d. J.T. Snow

7. No Giants player has ever won a Hank Aaron Award.

   a. True
   b. False

8. Which two Giants players split the 2016 Willie Mac Award?

   a. Brandon Crawford and Javier Lopez
   b. Matt Duffy and Javier Lopez
   c. Brandon Crawford and Madison Bumgarner
   d. Hunter Pence and Ryan Vogelsong

9. Which Giant won the 1996 Home Run Derby?

    a. Stan Javier

    b. Steve Scarsone

    c. Doug Mirabelli

    d. Barry Bonds

10. What year did Brian Sabean win TSN's MLB Executive of the Year Award?

    a. 2019

    b. 2003

    c. 2008

    d. 2016

11. Which Giant won the 1959 NL Rookie of the Year Award?

    a. Willie Mays

    b. Willie McCovey

    c. Orlando Cepeda

    d. Frank Linzy

12. Bruce Bochy NEVER won the NL Manager of the Year Award during his tenure with the Giants.

    a. True

    b. False

13. Which Giants player has NOT won an MLB Comeback Player of the Year Award?

    a. Buster Posey

    b. Barry Zito

    c. Willie McCovey

    d. Joe Morgan

14. What year was Willie McCovey named BOTH National League MVP and All-Star Game MVP?

    a. 1965
    b. 1969
    c. 1971
    d. 1967

15. What year did Willie Mays win BOTH an NL Gold Glove Award and the All-Star Game MVP Award?

    a. 1959
    b. 1970
    c. 1968
    d. 1965

16. Barry Bonds won five National League MVP Awards during his career with the Giants.

    a. True
    b. False

17. How many Gold Glove Awards did Matt Williams win during his tenure with the Giants?

    a. 8
    b. 1
    c. 3
    d. 5

18. Which Giant has NOT won the Willie Mac Award in back-to-back seasons?

    a. Mike Krukow
    b. Bengie Molina

c. Matt Cain

d. None of the above has won the award in back-to-back seasons.

19. Which Giants pitcher won a Silver Slugger Award in 2014 and 2015?

a. Matt Cain

b. Tim Lincecum

c. Tim Hudson

d. Madison Bumgarner

20. Willie Mays won a Roberto Clemente Award in 1971.

a. True

b. False

QUIZ ANSWERS

1. C – Buster Posey

2. B – False

3. D – Mike McCormick (1967)

4. B – Buster Posey

5. A – 3

6. C – Omar Vizquel

7. B – False, Buster Posey (2012)

8. A – Brandon Crawford and Javier Lopez

9. D – Barry Bonds

10. B – 2003

11. B – Willie McCovey

12. A – True

13. B – Barry Zito

14. B – 1969

15. C – 1968

16. A – True

17. C – 3

18. C – Matt Cain

19. D – Madison Bumgarner

20. A – True

DID YOU KNOW?

1. Madison Bumgarner was named MVP of both the NLCS and the World Series in 2014.

2. Buster Posey, Brandon Crawford, and Joe Panik all won NL Gold Glove Awards in 2016.

3. Marco Scutaro was named NLCS MVP in 2012.

4. Only two Giants players have won Cy Young Awards: Mike McCormick (1967) and Tim Lincecum (2008 and 2009).

5. Eleven Giants in franchise history have been named Rookie of the Year. They are Willie Mays (1951), Orlando Cepeda (1958), Willie McCovey (1959), Frank Linzy (1965), Dave Rader (1972), Gary Matthews (1973), John D'Acquisto (1974), John Montefusco (1975), Larry Herndon (1976), Robby Thompson (1986), and Buster Posey (2010). The Giants had a ROY each season from 1972-76.

6. Nine Giants players have been named National League MVP in 15 different seasons in franchise history. Those MVPs are Larry Doyle (1912), Bill Terry (1930), Carl Hubbell (1933 and 1936), Willie Mays (1964 and 1965), Willie McCovey (1969), Kevin Mitchell (1989), Barry Bonds (1993, 2001, 2002, 2003, and 2004), Jeff Kent (2000), and Buster Posey (2012).

7. Rod Beck won the NL Relief Man Award in 1994.

8. Four Giants execs have won the MLB Executive of the Year Award in franchise history: Horace Stoneham (1954), H.B. "Speck" Richardson (1978), Al Rosen (1987), and Brian Sabean (2003).

9. The very first winner of the Willie Mac Award was Jack Clark in 1980.

10. The first Giants player to win a Gold Glove was Willie Mays.

CHAPTER 16:

THE CITY

QUIZ TIME!

1. What is the name of the island that housed a prison from 1934 to 1963?

    c. Catalina Island

    d. Angel Island

    e. Alcatraz Island

    f. Treasure Island

2. The bear on the California flag lived in Golden Gate Park.

    a. True

    b. False

3. Which article of clothing was invented in San Francisco?

    a. Caftan

    b. Halter top

    c. Bathing suits

    d. Denim jeans

4. What is the name of the 210 ft. tower rising from the top of Telegraph Hill?

   a. Coit Tower
   b. Space Needle
   c. Willis Tower
   d. Eiffel Tower

5. Which famous band played their final concert at Candlestick Park in San Francisco?

   a. Queen
   b. The Beatles
   c. The Beach Boys
   d. Fleetwood Mac

6. What color is the Golden Gate Bridge?

   a. Orange
   b. Red
   c. Gold
   d. Black

7. There are eight sharp turns on Lombard Street.

   a. True
   b. False

8. What is the name of San Francisco's NFL team? (Even though they now play in Santa Clara, about 30 minutes away.)

   a. San Francisco Seals
   b. San Francisco Gold Rush

c. San Francisco Warriors

d. San Francisco 49ers

9. What is the name of San Francisco's NBA team? (They recently moved from Oakland.)

   a. San Francisco Kings

   b. San Francisco Warriors

   c. Golden State Warriors

   d. Golden State Kings

10. What kind of natural disaster caused severe damage to the city of San Francisco in 1906?

    a. Tornado

    b. Earthquake

    c. Hurricane

    d. Tsunami

11. Which of the following was NOT invented in San Francisco?

    a. Fortune cookies

    b. Bendy straws

    c. Jukebox

    d. Washing machine

12. San Francisco cable cars are the only national historical monument that can move.

    a. True

    b. False

13. What two colors did the U.S. Navy plan to paint the Golden Gate Bridge?

    a. Black with orange stripes
    b. Black with yellow stripes
    c. Red with yellow stripes
    d. Red with black stripes

14. What is San Francisco International Airport's code?

    a. SFO
    b. SFA
    c. SFI
    d. SFE

15. Back in 1835, San Francisco was originally called _____.

    a. Tiempo Buena
    b. Pueblo Brumoso
    c. Yerba Buena
    d. La Ciudad de las Focas

16. Most of San Francisco is built on top of buried Gold Rush ships.

    a. True
    b. False

17. Which of the following TV sitcoms was set in San Francisco?

    a. The Fresh Prince of Bel Air
    b. The King of Queens
    c. Modern Family
    d. Full House

18. Which chocolate company has a square named after it in Fisherman's Wharf?

   a. Hershey's
   b. Ghirardelli
   c. Dove
   d. Cadbury

19. What is the name of the two-deck bridge that connects San Francisco to Oakland?

   a. Coronado Bridge
   b. Benicia Bridge
   c. Bay Bridge
   d. Dumbarton Bridge

20. San Francisco outlawed burials in 1901.

   a. True
   b. False

QUIZ ANSWERS

1. C – Alcatraz Island

2. A – True

3. D – Denim jeans (Levi Strauss created them for Gold Rush miners.)

4. A – Coit Tower

5. B – The Beatles

6. A – Orange

7. A – True

8. D – San Francisco 49ers

9. C – Golden State Warriors

10. B – Earthquake

11. D – Washing machine

12. A – True

13. B – Black with yellow stripes

14. A – SFO

15. C – Yerba Buena (which translates to "Good Herb" from Spanish)

16. A – True

17. D – *Full House*

18. B – Ghirardelli

19. C – Bay Bridge

20. A – True

DID YOU KNOW?

1. Golden Gate Park is home to the de Young Museum, California Academy of Sciences, Japanese Tea Garden, Conservatory of Flowers, an aquarium, an arboretum, a playground, and more.

2. One of California's 21 missions is in San Francisco. Mission San Francisco de Asís is located on Delores Street.

3. The San Francisco Zoo is a 100-acre zoo that houses over 1,000 animals from 250 different species.

4. The many famous people from San Francisco include Dorothea Lange, Ansel Adams, Dianna Agron, Lisa Bonet, Benjamin Bratt, Margaret Cho, Carol Channing, Darren Criss, Robin Williams, Aisha Tyler, Sharon Stone, Natalie Wood, Patton Oswalt, Rob Schneider, Leslie Mann, Cheech Marin, and Jeffery Tambor, among others.

5. San Francisco and the surrounding Bay Area were terrorized by The Zodiac Killer in the 1960s and 1970s. The identity of the serial killer is still unknown.

6. Alcatraz Prison housed some of the most infamous criminals in history, including Al Capone and George "Machine Gun" Kelly. It was also the site of the most infamous prison escape in history: On the night of June 11-12, 1962, Frank Morris, Clarence Anglin, and John Anglin escaped into the Pacific Ocean on a raft made of raincoats. It is unknown to this day whether the three survived.

7. Irish coffee was not created in Ireland. It was actually created in San Francisco. It is still a popular coffee cocktail.

8. Angel Island is the largest island in San Francisco Bay. It served as the West Coast's immigration station from 1910 to 1940, winning the nickname of the "Ellis Island of the West."

9. No one from the Bay Area calls San Francisco, "San Fran"; they call it "The City."

10. On Pier 39, you can view sea lions sunbathing up close. You can even watch them on a webcam on Pier 39's website when you can't be there in person.

CHAPTER 17:

BARRY

QUIZ TIME!

1. Where was Barry Bonds born?

    a. Las Vegas, Nevada

    b. Riverside, California

    c. Portland, Oregon

    d. Denver, Colorado

2. Barry Bonds is Reggie Jackson's cousin.

    a. True

    b. False

3. Barry Bonds played for the San Francisco Giants for 15 seasons. He only played for one other MLB team in his career. What was that other team?

    a. Seattle Mariners

    b. New York Yankees

    c. Pittsburgh Pirates

    d. Chicago White Sox

4. What year was Barry Bonds born?

    a. 1971
    b. 1965
    c. 1964
    d. 1969

5. Barry Bonds holds the record for most intentional walks in MLB history. How many did he have in his career?

    a. 293
    b. 500
    c. 608
    d. 688

6. How many splash hits did Barry Bonds hit at Oracle Park?

    a. 68
    b. 35
    c. 30
    d. 0

7. Barry Bonds is in the National Baseball Hall of Fame.

    a. True
    b. False

8. Where did Barry Bonds attend college?

    a. Arizona State University
    b. University of Arizona
    c. UC-Riverside
    d. California State University, Fullerton

9. Where did Barry Bonds attend high school?

a. Riverside Poly High School

b. La Sierra High School

c. Junipero Serra High School

d. San Mateo High School

10. Barry Bonds served as a hitting coach for the _____ for one season.

a. Miami Marlins

b. San Francisco Giants

c. Pittsburgh Pirates

d. Los Angeles Angels of Anaheim

11. In 2002, Barry Bonds carried the torch at the Winter Olympics in _____.

a. Nagano, Japan

b. Vancouver, Canada

c. Turin, Italy

d. Salt Lake City, Utah

12. The Giants retired Barry Bonds's number 25 on August 11, 2018, before a game against his former team, the Pittsburgh Pirates.

a. True

b. False

13. What is Barry Bonds's current role with the Giants?

a. Special advisor to the CEO

b. Hitting coach

c. Special assistant to special operations

d. Special advisor to the general manager

14. Barry Bonds's father was a Major League Baseball player as well. Which of the following teams did Bobby Bonds NOT play for during his 14-season MLB career?

    a. San Francisco Giants
    b. California Angels
    c. Philadelphia Phillies
    d. New York Yankees

15. What year did Barry Bonds's playing career end?

    a. 2005
    b. 2010
    c. 2009
    d. 2007

16. Barry Bonds hit a home run on every date between April 1 and September 29 in his career, except for August 5. August 5 was the date his father Bobby homered on the most.

    a. True
    b. False

17. Barry Bonds holds the all-time MLB home run record. He passed Hank Aaron on the list in 2007. How many home runs did Barry Bonds hit during his career?

    a. 755
    b. 762
    c. 759
    d. 803

18. How many MLB All-Star Games was Barry Bonds named to during his career?

   a. 14
   b. 18
   c. 12
   d. 8

19. How many Gold Glove Awards did Barry Bonds win during his career?

   a. 5
   b. 2
   c. 8
   d. 10

20. Barry Bonds won 12 Silver Slugger Awards during his career.

   a. True
   b. False

QUIZ ANSWERS

1. B – Riverside, California

2. A – True

3. C – Pittsburgh Pirates

4. C – 1964

5. D – 688

6. B – 35

7. B – False, His steroid use has kept him from being named to the HOF.

8. A – Arizona State University

9. C – Junipero Serra High School

10. A – Miami Marlins

11. D – Salt Lake City, Utah

12. A – True

13. A – Special advisor to the CEO

14. C – Philadelphia Phillies

15. D – 2007

16. A – True

17. B – 762

18. A – 14

19. C – 8

20. A – True

DID YOU KNOW?

1. Barry Bonds started a charity in 1993 called the Barry Bonds Family Foundation. The mission of the foundation is "to encourage, promote and fund programs designed to improve the educational achievements, standard of living, and quality of life conditions for African-American youth within the Bay Area community."

2. Barry Bonds won an ESPN ESPY Award for "Male Athlete of the Year" in 1994.

3. After Bonds's playing career ended, he was investigated for use of steroids. He was put on trial and sentenced to two years of probation, 30 days of house arrest, and 250 hours of community service, and was charged a $4,000 fine.

4. Barry Bonds has made a few TV and movie appearances in his lifetime. He starred in the movies *Rookie of the Year* as himself. He also made TV appearances on *Beverly Hills 90210* and *Nash Bridges*.

5. Barry Bonds also played basketball and football in high school.

6. Barry Bonds was drafted by the Giants out of high school but decided to pass and attended Arizona State instead. He was then drafted by the Pirates out of college and made his way back to San Francisco in the end.

7. Barry Bonds graduated from Arizona State University in 1986 with a degree in criminology. He was named the ASU On Deck Circle Most Valuable Player. He was not well-liked by his Sun Devil teammates because he was self-centered.

8. Barry Bonds didn't retire from playing. The Giants announced they would not be re-signing him in 2008, and Bonds's agent responded, "I'm anticipating widespread interest from every Major League team." He never played in the MLB again.

9. Bonds was known for being difficult, ungrateful, and full of attitude. He has said that he now regrets his behavior and the way he treated the press. He claims he could have had more endorsements if he had behaved more kindly.

10. Bonds was the oldest player (38) to win the National League batting title when he did it in 2002.

CHAPTER 18:

STRETCH

QUIZ TIME!

1. Where was Willie McCovey born?

   a. Anchorage, Alaska
   b. Mobile, Alabama
   c. Tampa Bay, Florida
   d. Salt Lake City, Utah

2. Willie McCovey hit 521 home runs in his career, 231 of them in Candlestick Park, the most in that ballpark by any player.

   a. True
   b. False

3. What year did the San Francisco Giants retire Willie McCovey's number 44?

   a. 1988
   b. 1975
   c. 1980
   d. 1999

4. When was Willie McCovey born?

   a. January 10, 1938
   b. January 10, 1940
   c. November 8, 1938
   d. November 8, 1940

5. Willie McCovey played for three MLB teams in his 22-season career, all of them in California. Which California-based team did McCovey NOT play for?

   a. San Francisco Giants
   b. San Diego Padres
   c. Oakland Athletics
   d. Los Angeles Dodgers

6. What is the name of the section of the San Francisco Bay beyond right field at Oracle Park?

   a. McCovey Bay
   b. Willie's Ocean
   c. McCovey Cove
   d. Willie's Waters

7. Willie McCovey dropped out of high school to help his family financially.

   a. True
   b. False

8. What year was Willie McCovey inducted into the National Baseball Hall of Fame?

   a. 1986
   b. 1988

c. 1993

d. 1978

9. When did Willie McCovey pass away?

 a. Halloween 2016

 b. Halloween 2018

 c. Christmas 2016

 d. Christmas 2018

10. Which position did Willie McCovey NEVER hold within the Giants organization?

 a. Special assistant to the general manager

 b. Spring training instructor

 c. Hitting coach

 d. Senior advisor

11. How many MLB All-Star Games was Willie McCovey named to?

 a. 10

 b. 9

 c. 3

 d. 6

12. In 2018, Willie McCovey got married at Oracle Park.

 a. True

 b. False

13. What year did Willie McCovey win the National League Rookie of the Year Award?

 a. 1965

 b. 1955

c. 1959

d. 1960

14. What year was Willie McCovey named the National League MVP?

    a. 1969

    b. 1970

    c. 1961

    d. 1976

15. What year did Willie McCovey retire from the game of baseball?

    a. 1980

    b. 1983

    c. 1979

    d. 1975

16. Willie Mays and Willie McCovey notoriously disliked each other.

    a. True

    b. False

17. The Giants present an award named after McCovey each season to the player who is named the most inspirational by teammates, coaches, and staff. What is the name of that award?

    a. McCovey Award

    b. Willie McCovey Award

    c. Willie Mac Award

    d. W. McCovey Award

18. Which fellow MLB legend attended the same high school as Willie McCovey?

    a. Babe Ruth
    b. Hank Aaron
    c. Willie Mays
    d. Jackie Robinson

19. In 1996, McCovey and a former Giants teammate were charged with tax evasion for the money they earned selling autographs. Willie was put on probation and fined. He was later pardoned by which U.S. president?

    a. Bill Clinton
    b. George W. Bush
    c. Barack Obama
    d. Donald Trump

20. Although Willie McCovey has a whole cove named after him at Oracle Park, he never actually played in said park.

    a. True
    b. False

QUIZ ANSWERS

1. B – Mobile, Alabama

2. A – True

3. C – 1980

4. A – January 10, 1938

5. D – Los Angeles Dodgers

6. C – McCovey Cove

7. A – True

8. A – 1986

9. B – Halloween 2018

10. C – Hitting coach

11. D – 6

12. A – True

13. C – 1959

14. A – 1969

15. A – 1980

16. B – False

17. C – Willie Mac Award

18. B – Hank Aaron

19. C – Barack Obama

20. A – True, Oracle Park opened in 2000, 20 years after McCovey retired.

DID YOU KNOW?

1. Willie McCovey spent 19 years of his 22-year career with the San Francisco Giants. He started his career and ended it in San Francisco, coming full circle.

2. After retirement, Willie McCovey found a home in Woodside, California. The baseball field in Woodside was dedicated to him and named "Willie McCovey Field."

3. The Giants held a public memorial service for Willie McCovey at Oracle Park on November 8, 2018, following his death.

4. Willie McCovey was buried in a Giants casket with his number 44 on each side.

5. Keeping watch over McCovey Cove is a bronze statue of Willie McCovey. The area in which it is placed is called McCovey Point.

6. Willie McCovey had knee problems that left him in a wheelchair. He had several knee surgeries and several hospital stays due to arthritic hips, knees, and feet.

7. "Tonight, San Franciscans and baseball fans all across America mourn the passage of a true legend of the game. Willie McCovey was a titan on and off the field. From his humble beginnings in the segregated South to his induction to Major League Baseball's Hall of Fame, Willie McCovey lived the American Dream. He earned

international renown for his talent and leadership. For decades after he retired, Willie's community service earned the devotion of generations of San Franciscans. That the San Francisco Giants' annual most inspirational player award is named for Willie McCovey is a lasting testament to his joy, generosity of spirit, and optimism. We will carry Willie in our hearts and honor his memory every time the Giants drive a home run into McCovey Cove. May it be a comfort to Willie's wife Estela and the entire McCovey family that our whole city, and so many more across the country, join in mourning this extraordinary man." – Speaker of the House, Nancy Pelosi, following McCovey's passing.

8. Willie McCovey is buried at Cypress Lawn Memorial Park in Colma, California, a little over 10 miles from Oracle Park.

9. Willie McCovey was named the 1969 MLB All-Star Game MVP. His teammate, fellow Giants legend Willie Mays had won the MLB All-Star Game MVP Award the year before. A Giant did not win the award again until Bobby Bonds in 1973.

10. Willie McCovey was inducted into the Multi-Ethnic Sports Hall of Fame in Oakland, California, on February 7, 2009.

CONCLUSION

Learn anything new? Now you truly are the ultimate Giants fan. Not only did you learn about the Giants of the modern era, but you also expanded your knowledge back to the New York days.

You learned about the Giants' origins, the team's history and where it came from. You learned about the history of their uniforms and jersey numbers, you identified some famous quotes, and you read some of the craziest nicknames of all time. You learned more about the famous "Say Hey" Willie Mays, the legendary Willie McCovey, and the controversial but powerful Barry Bonds. You learned some Giants stats and recalled some of the biggest Giants trades and drafts. You broke down your knowledge by outfielders, infielders, pitchers, and catchers. You looked back on the Giants' World Series wins and the awards that came before, after, and during them. You also learned about the Giants' fiercest rivalries of all time including the Los Angeles Dodgers, Oakland A's, and New York Yankees.

Every team in the MLB has a storied history, but the Giants have one of the longest. Living through a 52-year World

Series drought takes some dedicated fans. Being the ultimate Giants fan takes a lot of knowledge and patience, which you tested with this book. Whether you knew every answer or were stumped by many of the questions, you learned about one of the most incredible histories that the game of baseball has to offer.

The history of the Giants represents what we all love about the game of baseball: the heart, the determination, the tough times, and the unexpected moments, plus the players that inspire us and encourage us to do our best because, even if you get knocked down, there is always another game and another day.

With players like Buster Posey, Brandon Crawford, and Madison Bumgarner, the future for the Giants looks bright. There is no doubt that this franchise will continue to be one of the most recognized sports teams in America.

It's a new decade, which means there is a clean slate, ready to continue writing the history of the San Francisco Giants. The ultimate Giants fan cannot wait to see what's to come for their Boys by the Bay.

Printed in the USA
CPSIA information can be obtained
at www.ICGtesting.com
LVHW020850261223
767355LV00004B/334